Disney's POCAHONTAS
NATURE GUIDE
Woods and Wildlife

BY GINA INGOGLIA, ASLA

ILLUSTRATED BY GINA INGOGLIA AND JOSÉ CARDONA

Disney PRESS

NEW YORK

© 1995 by Disney Press.

All rights reserved. No part of this book may be reproduced or transmitted in any form or by any means, electronic or mechanical, including photocopying, recording, or by any information storage and retrieval system, without permission from the publisher. For information address Disney Press, 114 Fifth Avenue, New York, New York 10011-5690.

Printed in the United States of America.

First Edition
1 3 5 7 9 10 8 6 4 2

The artwork for each picture is prepared using pencil.
This book is set in 12-point Caslon 540

Library of Congress Catalog Card Number: 95-70030
ISBN: 0-7868-4055-2

Printed on recycled paper.

Contents

INTRODUCTION 4

WHITE ASH 8
BASSWOOD 10
PAPER BIRCH 12
BUTTERNUT 14
WESTERN RED CEDAR 16
FLOWERING DOGWOOD 18

SLIPPERY ELM 20
COCKSPUR HAWTHORN 22
SHAGBARK HICKORY 24
SUGAR MAPLE 26
RED OAK 28
EASTERN WHITE PINE 30

What Is a Tree? 7
What's Its Real Name? 32
How Leaves Change Color 33
What Good Are Trees? 34
Leaves 36
Tree Flowers and Fruits 38
A Close Look at Bark and What's Behind It 40
Become a Tree Detective 42
Tree Dwellers 45
Who's Hiding on the Floor? 47
Tracks in the Snow 48
That's a Snowflake? 49
Wildflowers 50
Fern: Two Plants in One 52
Mushrooms: They Can't Live Alone! 53
Birds, Birds, Birds! 54
Trees Today . . . 56
. . . And Tomorrow 57
Tips for the Nature Trail 60
Index 62

One day Pocahontas paddled down the river and floated into a shady forest glade. She climbed out of her canoe and sat beside Grandmother Willow.

"The birds are singing so sweetly this morning, my child," the ancient tree told Pocahontas. "They must be happy to see you!"

"Well, I'm happy to listen," said Pocahontas. "I think birds are what I like the best about the forest."

Grandmother Willow smiled. "Oh, really? What about the silent deer, the powerful bear, the tiny bee, and all the other creatures?" she asked.

Pocahontas smiled back. "I like them the best as well!"

"And the flowers?" asked Grandmother Willow. "What would we do without them?"

"Oh, yes," Pocahontas agreed, "flowers brighten up the cloudiest day and fill the air with sweet fragrance. I suppose there is no *best* part of the forest. The birds, the other creatures, the flowers—they're all special."

"Aren't you forgetting something?" Grandmother Willow asked. "What about the trees?"

Pocahontas laughed. "Of course I haven't forgotten the trees. You already know I love them. There would be no forest at all without the beautiful trees."

"But you must also remember," said Grandmother Willow, "trees are not just nice to look at. People need trees. They make use of the wood and bark, the fruits, saps, and seeds, even the tangled roots growing beneath the ground."

Grandmother Willow gently touched Pocahontas with one of her long trailing branches.

"With the help of Sun and Rain—," she said, "the people, the trees, and the creatures who dwell here—we all share Mother Earth under the watchful eye of our Father the Sky."

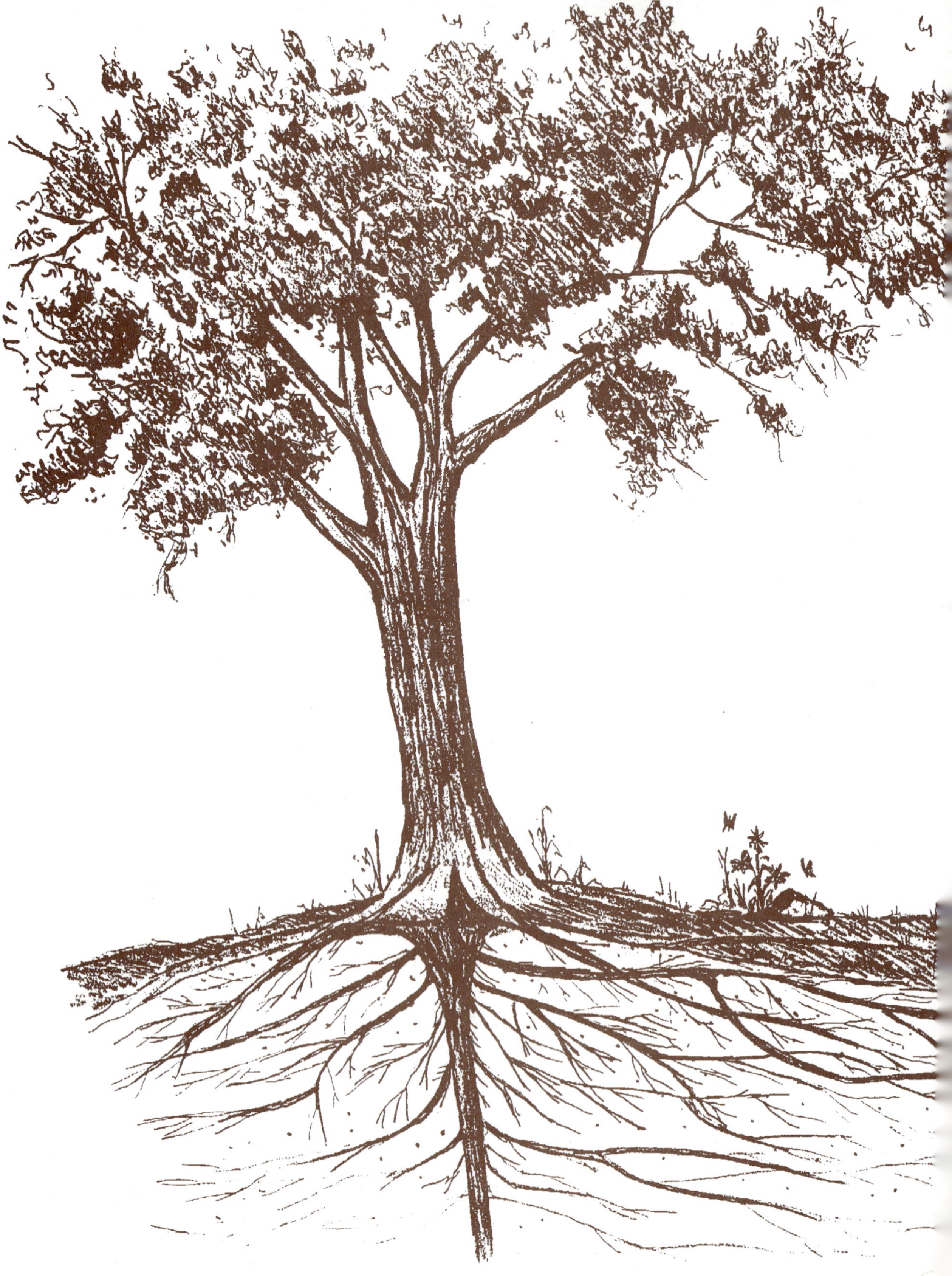

What Is a Tree?

Trees are the biggest plants of all. Like people and animals, they need food and water to stay alive. They get their nourishment from their own leaves and roots.

Leaves contain a green substance called chlorophyll (KLOR-oh-fill). When the sun shines on the leaves, the chlorophyll begins to work. It changes moisture and gases in the air into sugars. This process is called photosynthesis (foe-toe-SIN-theh-sis). The sugars feed the tree by moving from the leaves, throughout the branches, and down the trunk to the roots.

The roots provide the tree with water. After rainwater seeps down underground, thready root hairs soak it up. The rainwater dissolves underground minerals and salts (more tree food!). The roots soak them up as well. The roots change the water into root sap. The nourishing sap moves from the roots, up the trunk, throughout the branches, and out to the leaves.

Of course, roots are important for another reason: they tie the tree to the ground so it doesn't topple over.

The following twelve trees are all species that were found in the United States at the time that Pocahontas lived. After that, you'll find some more information that you can use to help explore the woods and wildlife of today.

White Ash

When a field is left untended, a tree will often spring up from the grass. One of the first trees to appear is usually the white ash. It grows quickly, gaining about two feet in height every year. Usually when trees grow so fast their wood isn't very strong. But this isn't true of the white ash. Its wood is strong and hard and can take rough treatment.

The white ash's fruits are papery thin and look a bit like tiny airplane propellers. They are called samaras (suh-MAR-ahs). In the fall, they hang in bunches until they drop off or the wind blows them away.

Almost all tree trunks grow in layers called growth rings. When the white ash is cut into logs, its layers can be separated if the log is stripped of its bark and pounded. Woodland people took advantage of this. After they pounded and stripped off the layers (called splints), they trimmed and split them into long narrow strips. Then they wove the splints into useful baskets.

WHITE ASH
Fraxinus americana
(FRAX-ih-nuss am-er-ih-CANE-ah)

Can grow 50 to 80 feet tall.

Grows in valleys and forests in most of eastern United States.

SEED

LEAF
Dark green above, paler below in summer. Fall color: Yellow, deep purple, and maroon.

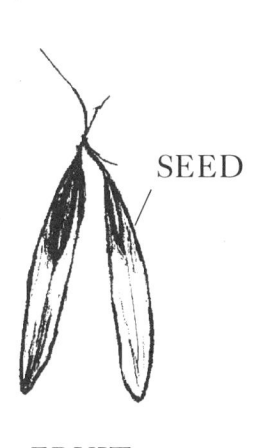

FRUIT
Samara

9

Basswood

On a June day, if you find a tall tree that's buzzing with bees, it might very well be a basswood. Its nickname is the bee-tree because bees like the nectar of this tree's flower so much. Many people think the honey that comes from the basswood is the finest in the world.

In springtime, tiny creamy-white flowers dangle from the middle of a leaflike structure called a bract (BRAKT). In the fall, nutlike fruits hang from the bract. The bract remains on the tree until the leaves fall off in autumn.

The basswood's wood is easy to carve. Some eastern woodlands people carved masks called false faces right on the trunks of living trees. Only very skilled artists were allowed to carve them. It was important that the basswood was alive, because the people believed that the spirit of the living tree became part of the false face. The carvers blew tobacco smoke into the roots and branches, believing it would cause the tree to heal and not die. After the false face was cut from the trunk, it was usually painted red or black.

BASSWOOD
Tilia americana
(TILL-ee-ah am-er-ih-CANE-ah)
Also called American linden or bee-tree

Usually grows 60 to 80 feet tall. Sometimes reaches 100 feet.

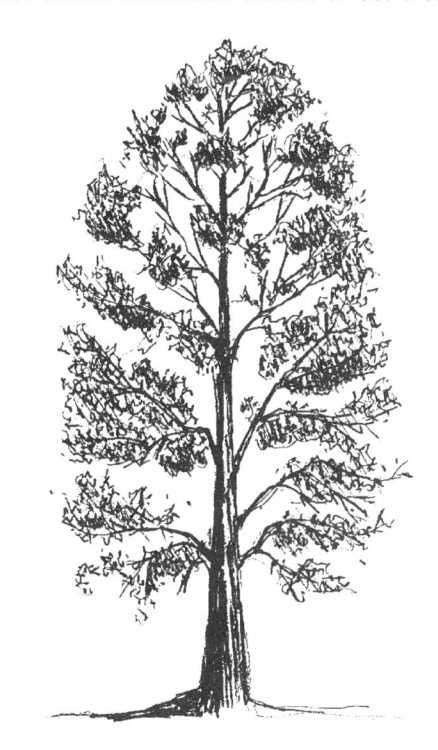

Grows in northeastern and midwestern United States.

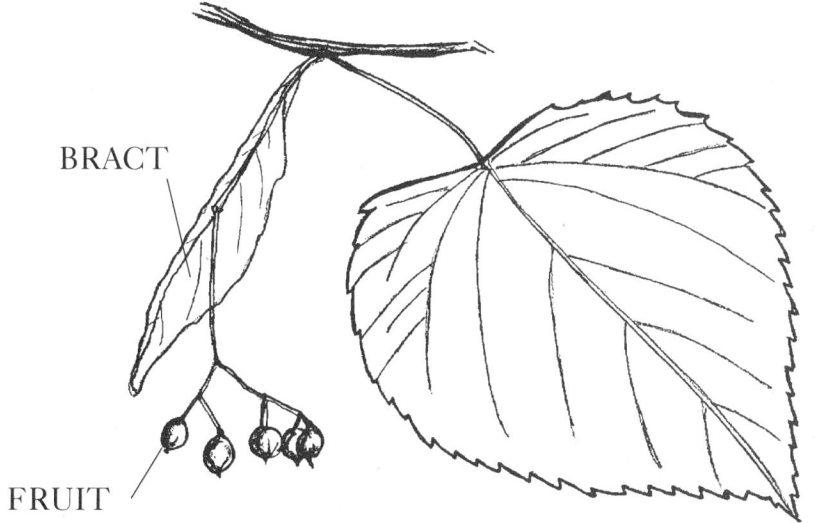

BRACT

FRUIT

LEAF
Dark green above, pale green below in summer. Fall color: Pale yellow or brown.

11

Paper Birch

It's easy to spot a paper birch. The white bark stands out even from a distance.

But the bark isn't always white. When the tree is young and small the trunk is a yellowish brown. As the tree grows the bark turns white and, in time, develops black markings. It also peels away in thin papery strips, curling up at the ends to reveal a reddish orange inner bark.

The bark has two other very interesting characteristics: it's very light in weight and it's waterproof. This makes it an ideal material for boatbuilding.

Native Americans in the north built birch-bark canoes in early summer. During that season the bark could be removed more easily without harming the tree. The men fitted large sheets of bark over wooden frames, and the women stitched them together with tree roots. The gaps were sealed with pitch, a sticky substance made from tree sap. And if it grew too dark to see before the canoe was finished, the people simply rolled up some bark into a tube and lit it, thereby creating a fine torch. It didn't even matter if it started to rain—birch bark burns even when it's wet!

PAPER BIRCH
Betula papyrifera
(BET-u-lah pap-ee-RIFF-er-ah)
Also called canoe birch or white birch

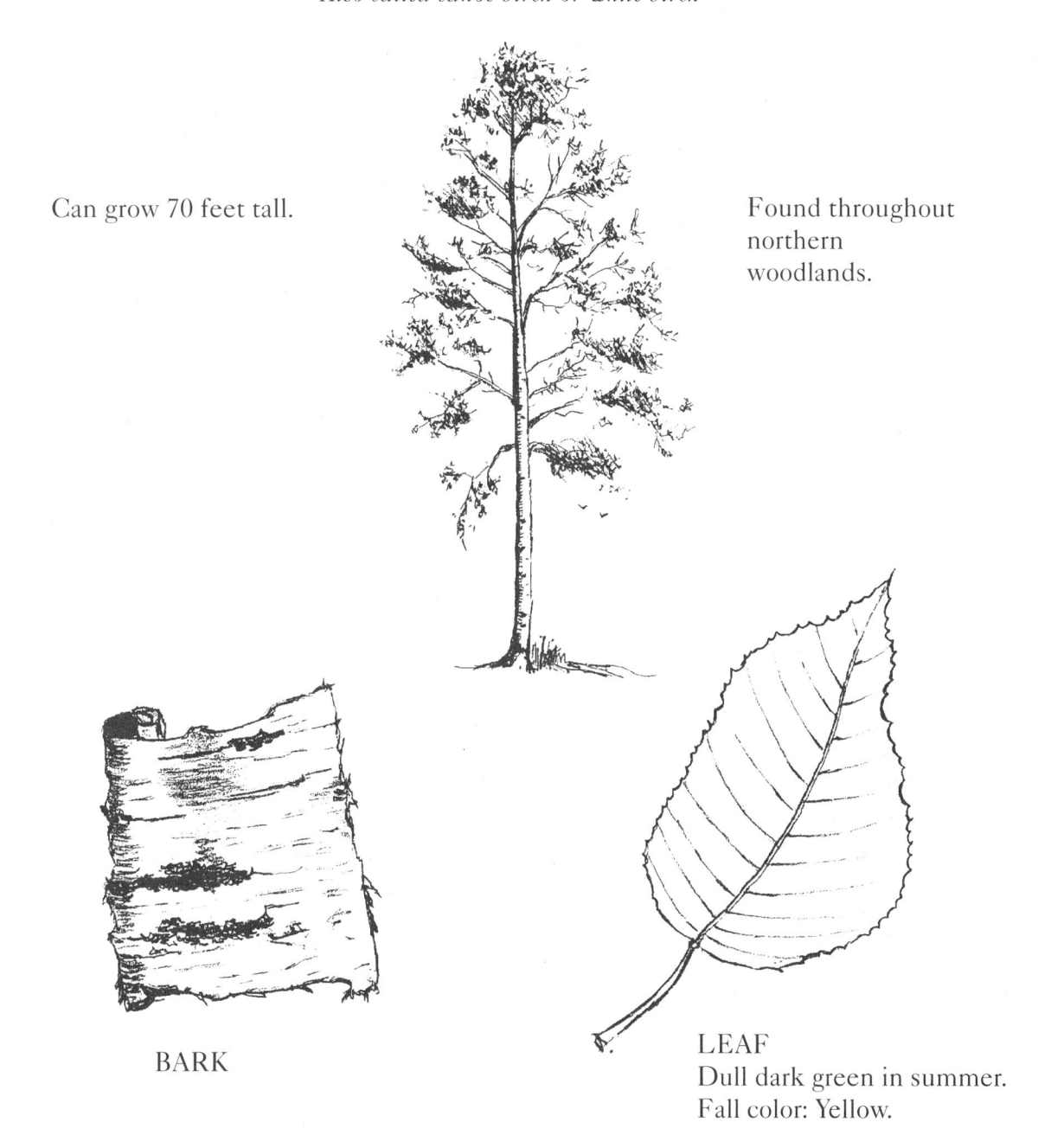

Can grow 70 feet tall.

Found throughout northern woodlands.

BARK

LEAF
Dull dark green in summer.
Fall color: Yellow.

Butternut

The butternut can grow in lots of different places. You might find one in a moist part of the woods and another growing in dry, rocky soil.

The tree's fruit is rust colored and shaped a bit like an egg. It contains a very oily seed called a butternut. Butternuts taste sweet, but they turn rancid (spoil) in a short time. So they have to be picked and eaten right away. When you handle a butternut's husk (outer covering) your fingers will turn brown.

Native Americans made dyes from plants. Different colors were obtained from different kinds of trees. Sometimes they dyed rushes (grasses) to be woven into mats. To dye them black, they boiled the inner bark of the butternut together with unripe nuts of the hazelnut tree. After the rushes were dipped into the boiling mixture for a short time, they were hung up and dried. This was done every day for two weeks. When they dried the right shade of black, the rushes were rubbed with fat to make them bendable. Then they could be woven with undyed rushes to create black patterns in the mats.

BUTTERNUT
Juglans cinerea
(JU-glanz sin-er-EE-ah)
Also called white walnut or oilnut

Grows 40 to 70 feet tall.

Found in forests of the northeastern, midwestern, and southern United States.
Prefers moist or rocky soils.

LEAF
Dark green in summer.
Fall color: Yellow or brown.

FRUIT

SEED
(Butternut)

15

Western Red Cedar

The western red cedar is a tough-wooded evergreen tree with thick, stringy bark. *Evergreen* means the leaves stay on all year long. Red cedar leaves are unusual—they look like little braided needles. If you pinch them between your fingers, you might think they smell a lot like pineapple.

For hundreds of years, Native Americans living on the rainy northwest coast found good uses for red cedar bark and roots. For protection from the wet weather, they twined the bark into capes and tightly woven hats. And because the roots were so tough, they became handy fishhooks.

Most important of all, the coastland dwellers carved the wood into something very special—after removing the bark, they carved the red cedars into totem poles.

Totem poles are some of the tallest wooden sculptures in the world. They were created to stand as signs of welcome to a village or were placed at the entrance to a house. Many were erected in memory of the dead.

Each totem figure (often an animal) represented a part of a story. Because storytellers were important people in village life, the totem poles were respected and honored, too. Today in the Northwest, skilled Native American artists are carving totem poles once again.

WESTERN RED CEDAR
Thuja plicata
(THOO-yah plih-KATE-ah)
Also called giant arborvitae (arbor-VY-tee)

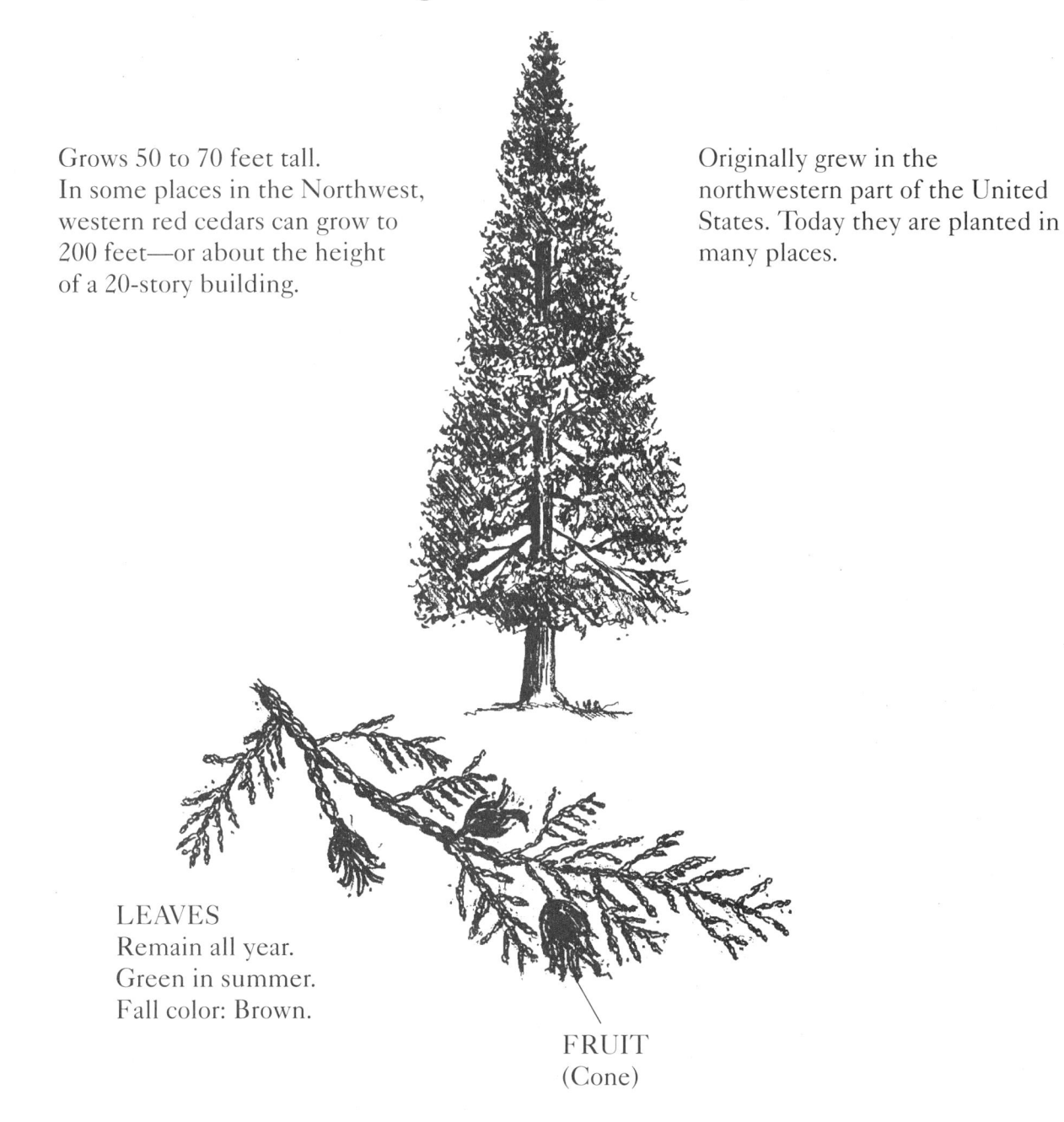

Grows 50 to 70 feet tall. In some places in the Northwest, western red cedars can grow to 200 feet—or about the height of a 20-story building.

Originally grew in the northwestern part of the United States. Today they are planted in many places.

LEAVES
Remain all year.
Green in summer.
Fall color: Brown.

FRUIT
(Cone)

Flowering Dogwood

The dogwood is a small tree with low branches. It often grows in the dappled shade of towering forest trees. Dogwoods don't need strong sunshine to flower, and their white blooms brighten the woods in April and May.

But what you think are showy petals aren't really flowers at all. If you look closely at each blossom you can see the actual flowers. They are tiny, greenish yellow, and grow in clusters in the middle. The four white "petals" are called bracts (BRAKTS), which are leafy parts of the plant.

In the fall the dogwood bears glossy red fruits that look like tiny footballs. Sometimes they stay on the branches until December. But they are usually gobbled up by hungry birds first.

For centuries woodland people discovered medicines in many kinds of plants. The dogwood was one of them. Its bark and roots were used to treat various diseases. Today scientists are still searching for ways to make new medicines from plants, just as people did with the dogwood long ago.

FLOWERING DOGWOOD
Cornus florida
(KOR-nuss FLAHR-ih-dah)

Can grow 20 or 30 feet tall.

Grows throughout the eastern United States.

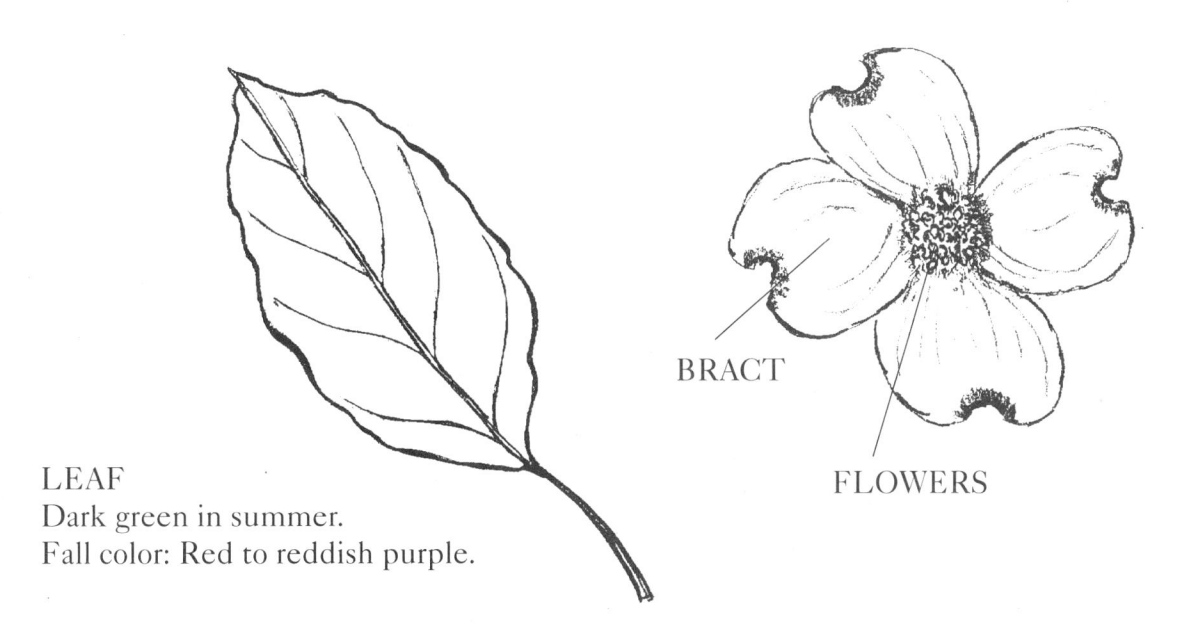

BRACT

FLOWERS

LEAF
Dark green in summer.
Fall color: Red to reddish purple.

Slippery Elm

The slippery elm is a medium-size tree with leaves that are easy to identify. The upper surfaces are very rough and feel like sandpaper; the undersides are hairy. The tree's twigs and buds are also rough and covered with little red hairs.

A slippery elm fruit is smaller than a thumbnail. It's called a samara (suh-MAR-ah). The samara is made up of two smooth papery-thin wings, joined together to almost form a circle. There is a hairy seed in the center.

The slippery elm gets its name from its slimy inner bark. People living in the wild chewed it when they were thirsty.

Early forest dwellers removed this tree's bark in sheets from springtime to early July, when it was easiest to separate from the trunk, attaching it to wooden frames to construct bark lodges for summer use.

In the snowy north, Native American boys and girls had fun in wintertime with sheets of slippery elm bark. After turning up one end and tying a rope to it, they stood on the bark, held on to the rope, and coasted down snowy hills.

SLIPPERY ELM
Ulmus rubra
(ULL-mus ROO-bra)
Also called red elm or moose elm

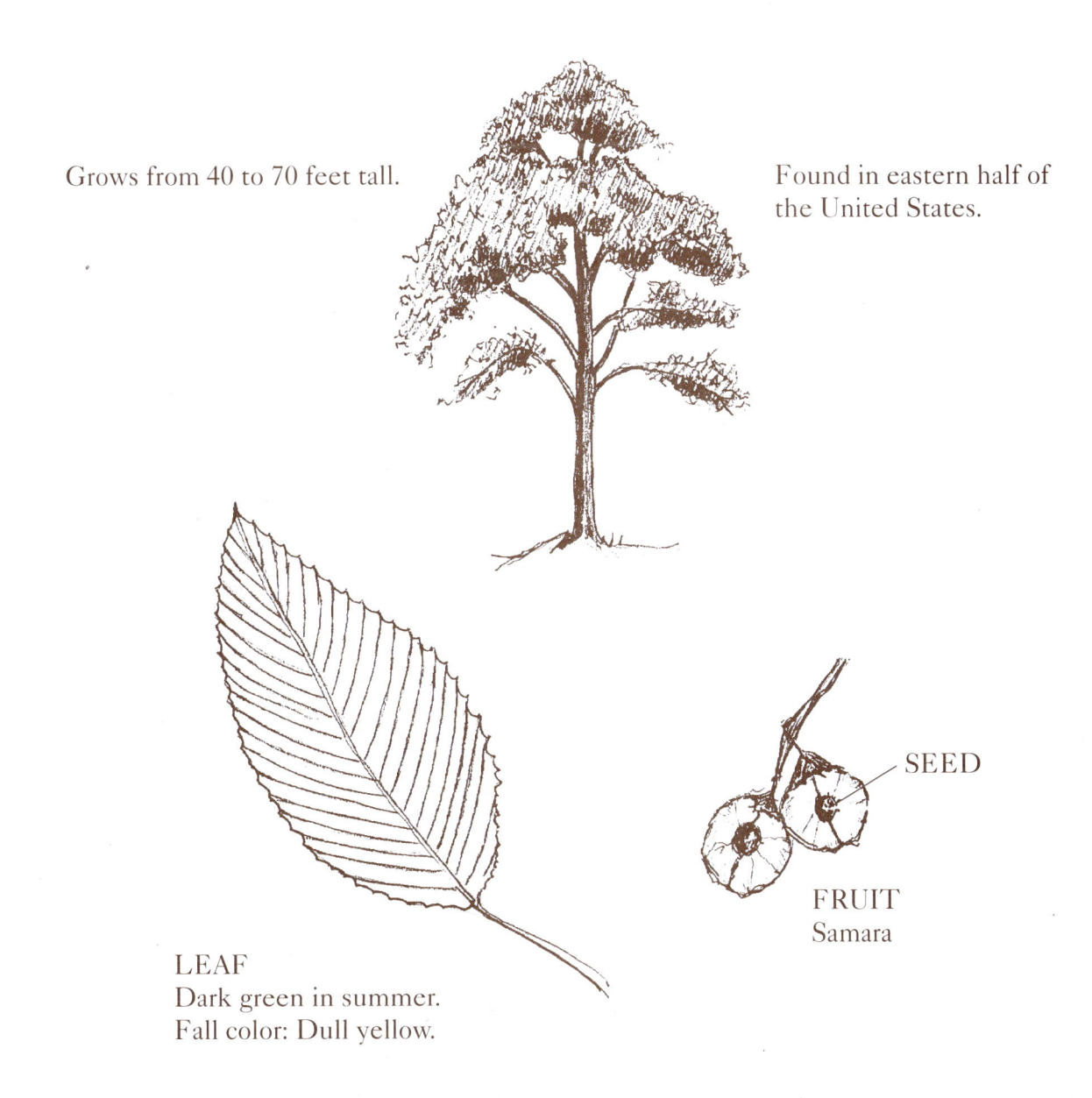

Grows from 40 to 70 feet tall.

Found in eastern half of the United States.

LEAF
Dark green in summer.
Fall color: Dull yellow.

SEED

FRUIT
Samara

Cockspur Hawthorn

There's one important thing to remember about the cockspur hawthorn—watch out! It's covered with sharp, strong curved thorns up to three inches long.

In late spring or early summer cockspur hawthorns are covered with pretty white flowers. The leaves have toothed edges. By late September or October, small dark-red fruits droop from the branches. Because most birds don't like to eat them, hawthorn fruits stay on the tree until springtime.

Native Americans found the long sharp thorns came in handy. They used them as pins and awls. An awl is a tool that pokes holes in leather and stiff material. Many deerskin clothes and moccasins were sewn with the help of hawthorn awls.

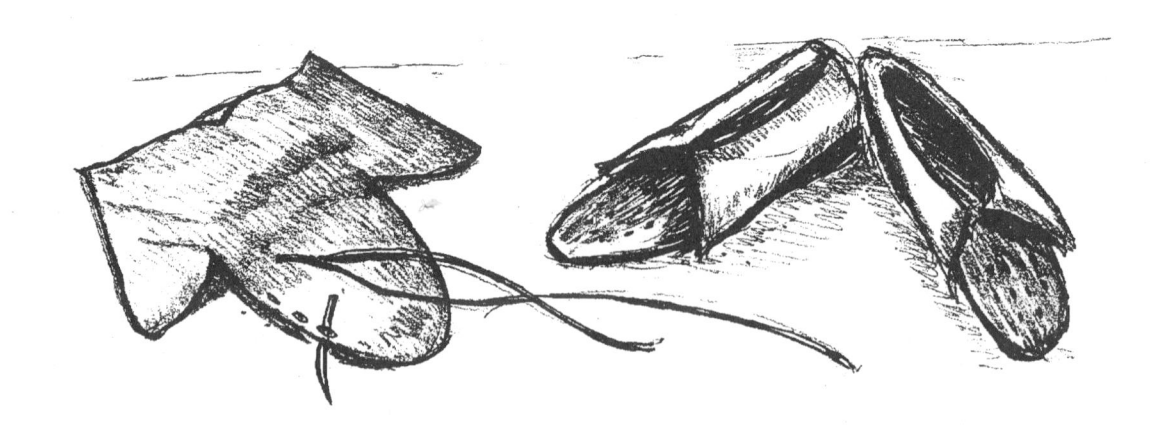

COCKSPUR HAWTHORN
Crataegus crus-galli
(cra-TEE-gus croos-GAL-lee)

Grows 20 to 30 feet tall.

Found in moist soils in the eastern half of the United States.

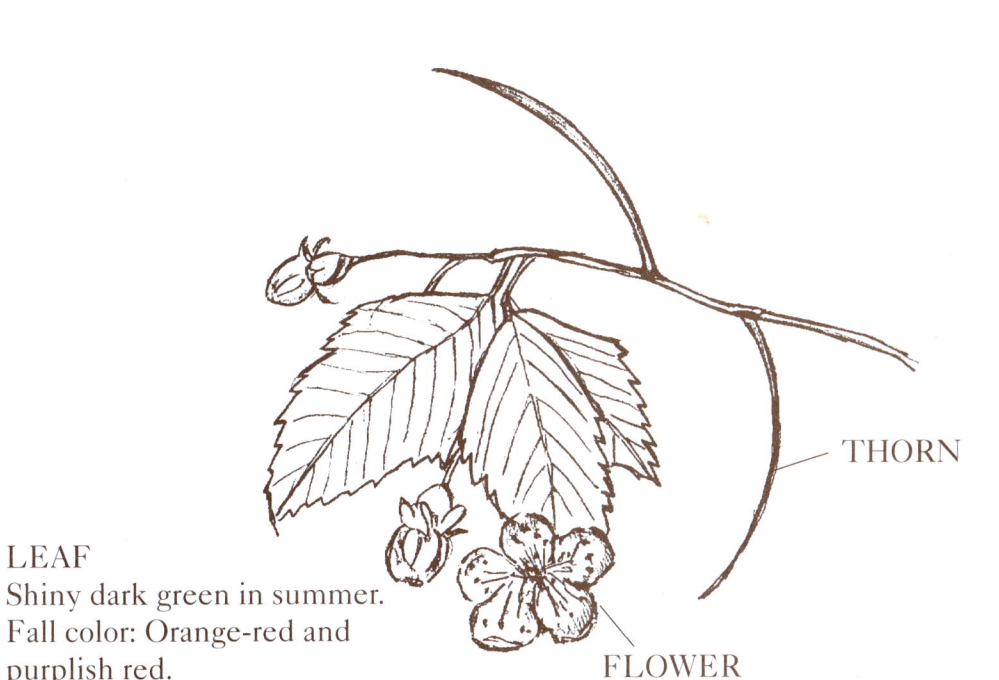

THORN

LEAF
Shiny dark green in summer.
Fall color: Orange-red and purplish red.

FLOWER

Shagbark Hickory

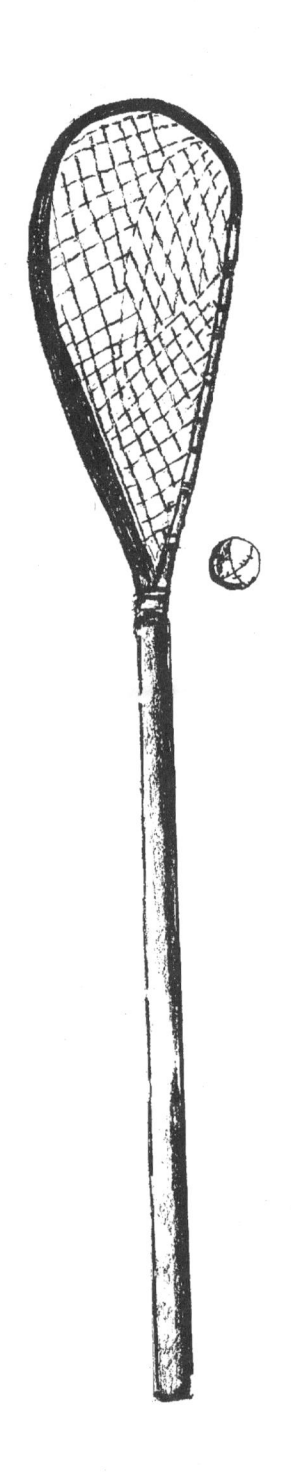

The shagbark hickory is well named. On old trees, the bark breaks away by itself and sticks out from the trunk, giving the trunk a shaggy look.

The leaves are large. Each leaf is divided into five smaller leaflets, making it look like five leaves instead of one. Leaves that are divided in this way are called compound leaves.

The tree's dark brown fruit is roundish in shape. The nut inside contains a seed or kernel (the part of the nut that you eat). *Hickory* is from an Algonquian word for the oily sweet milk made from the nut. Hickory was prepared by soaking and boiling the kernels. When the boiled kernels were pounded, the milk oozed out of them.

Native Americans also made lacrosse sticks from the strong hickory wood. Lacrosse is a sport that woodland people played centuries before Europeans discovered America. Today lacrosse is a team sport played in schools all over the United States.

SHAGBARK HICKORY
Carya ovata
(KAY-ree-ah oh-VAY-tah)

Usually grows 60 to 80 feet tall. Some reach 120 feet.

Found in forests in eastern half of United States.

LEAF
Deep yellow-green in summer. Fall color: Deep yellow and golden brown.

FRUIT

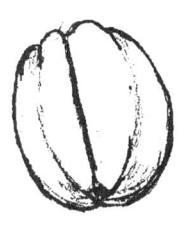

NUT

Sugar Maple

Each year people from all over the world travel to New England to see the colorful autumn leaves. The sugar maples, with shining orange, red, and yellow leaves, are among the most beautiful trees of all.

You can also see the paper-thin sugar maple fruit in the fall. They are called samaras (suh-MAR-ahs). When the breeze blows, the samaras whirl to the ground like tiny helicopters.

Many people like sugar maples for another reason—these trees give us maple syrup. Hundreds of years ago, people living in northeastern woods figured out how to make maple syrup from sap. In late winter when the sap began to flow inside the tree trunk, they slashed the bark, inserted a flat piece of wood under it, and placed a container, often made from birch bark, beneath it. Slowly the watery sap ran down the wood, dripping into the container. The sap was taken inside a birch-bark lodge, where it was boiled until it thickened into maple syrup. Woodland people also made maple sugar for candy, cooking, and to sweeten drinks.

SUGAR MAPLE
Acer saccharum
(A-sir SACK-uh-rum)
Also called hard maple or rock maple

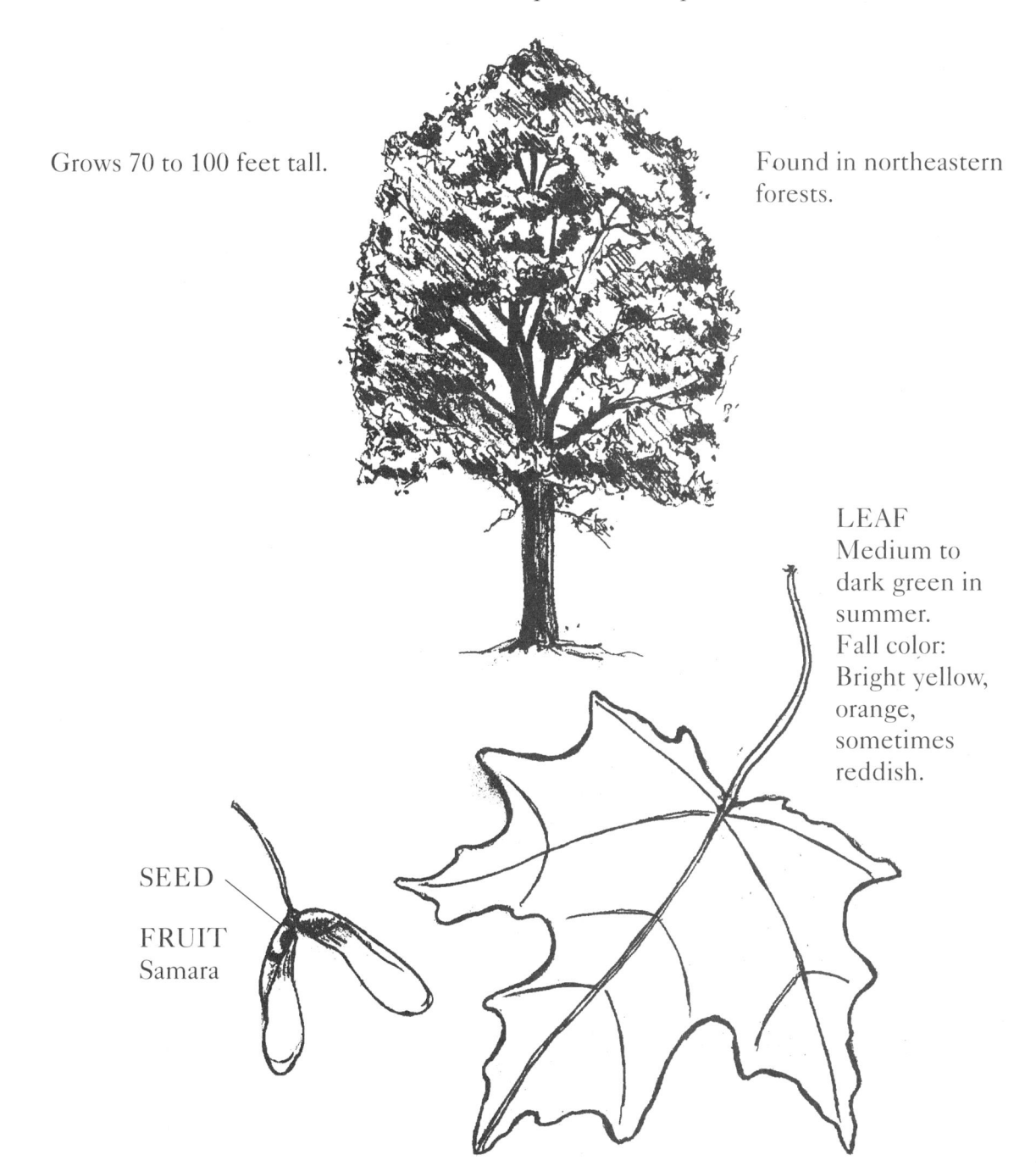

Grows 70 to 100 feet tall.

Found in northeastern forests.

LEAF
Medium to dark green in summer.
Fall color: Bright yellow, orange, sometimes reddish.

SEED

FRUIT Samara

Red Oak

When you see acorns on the ground, you're sure to find an oak tree nearby. Acorns are the oak's fruit. They are a favorite food of bears, white-tailed deer, and many other woodland creatures. Each year squirrels bury millions of acorns to last them though the cold winters. Of course, not all the acorns get eaten, so some sprout and grow into new trees.

Forest people often prepared foods from acorns. They had many ways of doing this. One way was to boil the acorns, split them open, and remove the kernel (the meaty part inside). Then the kernels were dried and mashed into a flour. The flour was often carried on trips. When travelers were hungry, they mixed the flour with water, and it turned into a nourishing mush. Sometimes they added berries or maple syrup—like you add sugar to hot cereal. Later, American pioneers often ate acorn mush.

RED OAK
Quercus rubra
(QUER-cuss ROO-brah)

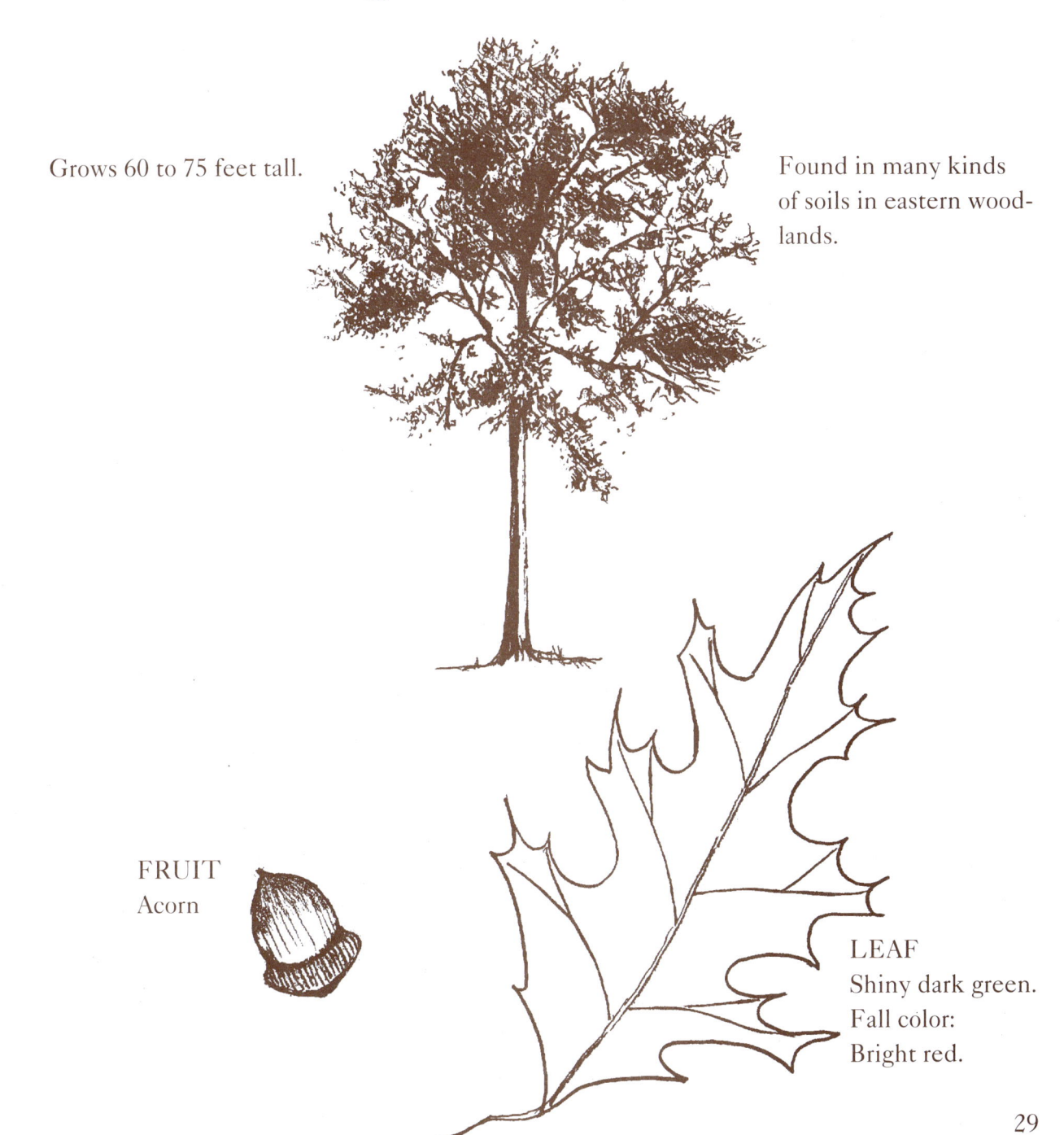

Grows 60 to 75 feet tall.

Found in many kinds of soils in eastern woodlands.

FRUIT
Acorn

LEAF
Shiny dark green.
Fall color:
Bright red.

Eastern White Pine

The eastern white pine grows very straight and tall. When the tree is old, much of the trunk is branchless. But when young it has a completely different shape—the branches grow up and down the whole trunk.

A pine fruit is called a cone. Tucked inside are seeds or pine nuts, which animals and people like to eat. The grayish green leaves look like long needles. In the fall many drop off. But most stay on the tree all year round.

Look closely at the needles. Several are joined at the base. This little cluster is called a fascicle (FAS-ih-cull). Depending upon the kind of pine, fascicles are made up of two, three, or five needles. Unless it has been damaged, there are always five needles in the fascicle of an eastern white pine.

Native Americans used slender pine trunks as tepee poles. After peeling off the bark and shaving them down, the men put up the poles. Then the women covered them with animal hides, which they often painted with designs.

EASTERN WHITE PINE
Pinus strobus
(PIE-nuss STROW-buss)

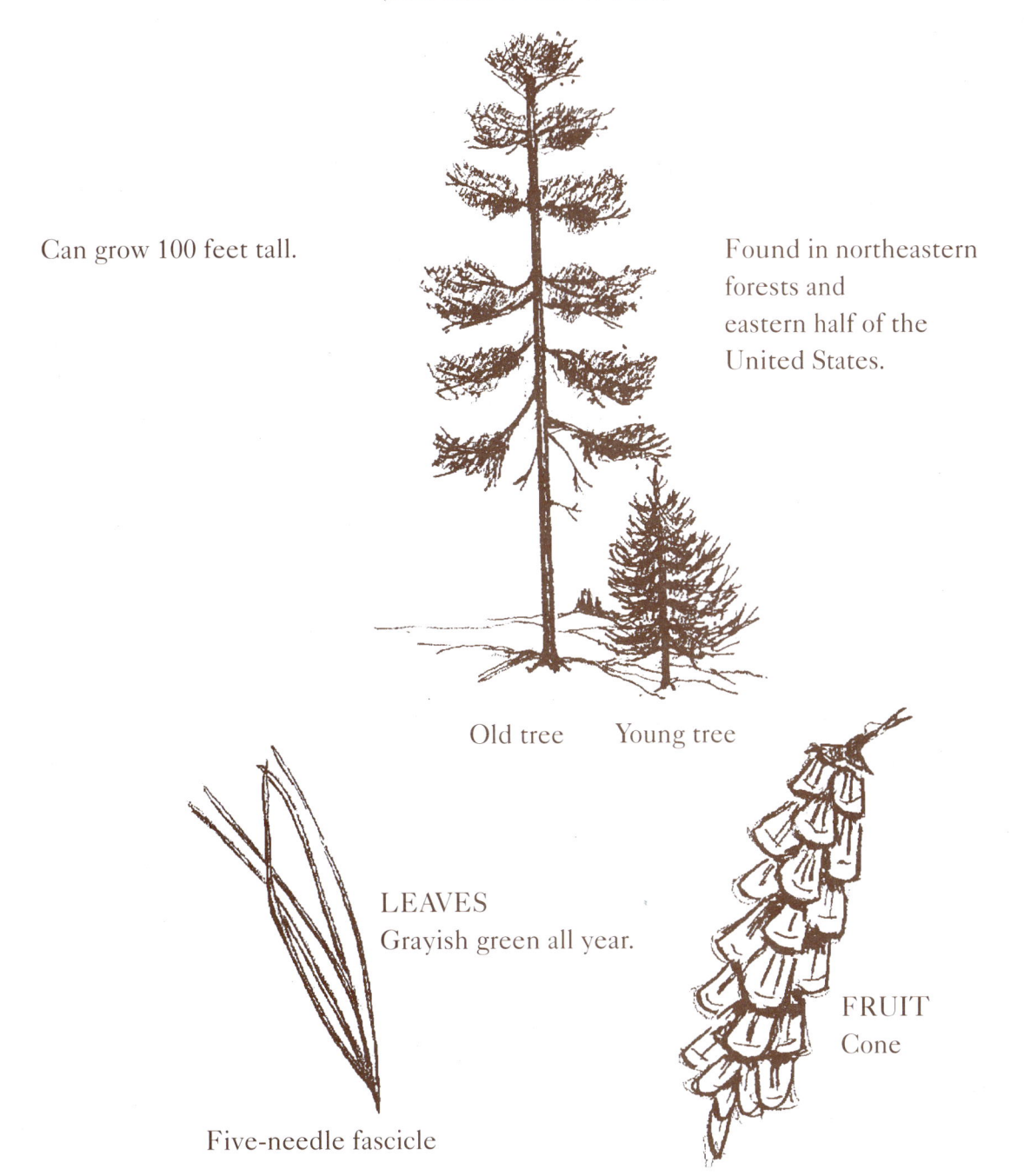

Can grow 100 feet tall.

Found in northeastern forests and eastern half of the United States.

Old tree   Young tree

LEAVES
Grayish green all year.

Five-needle fascicle

FRUIT
Cone

What's Its Real Name?

Every tree has two kinds of names—a common name and a scientific name.

Common names are easy to learn and remember—like basswood, paper birch, and white ash. But some trees have more than one common name: the paper birch is also called a canoe birch; the basswood is sometimes known as the bee-tree or the American linden.

To avoid confusion, each kind of tree has one scientific name. Since the scientific name is in Latin, it's often harder to learn and remember.

So a tree may be called a paper birch in one place and a canoe birch somewhere else. But its scientific name, *Betula papyrifera* (BET-u-lah pap-ee-RIFF-er-ah), is always the same, *all over the world*.

How Leaves Change Color

In places with cold winters, many trees lose all their leaves in the fall. But before dropping to the ground, the leaves often turn shades of yellow, orange, red, and purple.

Leaves contain yellow and orange pigments called carotenoids (ca-ROT-ten-oyds). You can't see them because they're covered up by a pigment or color called chlorophyll (KLOR-oh-fill). Chlorophyll makes the leaf look green.

When the weather grows cool, the chlorophyll breaks down and disappears. The carotenoids stay behind. Now the leaf looks yellow.

What about leaves that turn red or purple?

These colors come from pigments called anthocyanins (an-tho-SIGH-uh-nins). They aren't made until the fall. And they are made only in certain kinds of trees.

Anthocyanins are brightest when the fall weather is just right. The days must be sunny and not too hot or cold. The nights have to be very cold.

Some kinds of trees have just one fall color. Others have many. The combinations of pigments make up all the different shades. Now when you look at fall leaves you can say, "Wow, that tree made lots of anthocyanins!" or "Now I can see the carotenoids!"

SUGAR MAPLE— Red, orange, yellow

HORNBEAM— Orange, red

TULIP TREE— Yellow

SCARLET OAK— Red

GINKGO— Yellow

SASSAFRAS— Yellow, orange, red, purple

SWEETGUM— Yellow, purple, red

HONEYLOCUST— Yellow

What Good Are Trees?

Trees are such beautiful plants that they make the world a nicer place just by being around. But they also do a great deal more than that.

People and animals must breathe in a gas called oxygen (OX-eh-gin) to stay alive. They breathe out a gas called carbon dioxide (CAR-bon dy-OX-ide). Tree leaves take in carbon dioxide and give off oxygen.

Leaves give off water vapor that makes the air cooler on hot summer days. They also block out the hot sun and give us shade. And they trap pollen and dust, which cuts down on air pollution.

Tree roots hold the soil in place. During heavy rains they keep the ground from washing away. This helps prevent floods and landslides.

Farmers protect their crops by planting rows of trees called windbreaks. By lessening the force of strong winds, windbreaks prevent soil from blowing way.

These are just a few of the ways that trees help us—and why we should take care of them.

Leaves

The "leafy" part of a leaf is the blade. A simple leaf has just one blade. The blade is often attached to a twig by a leaf stem called the petiole (PET-ee-ole).

The blades in some leaves are divided up into many leaflets. This is called a compound leaf. It may look like many leaves but it's only one.

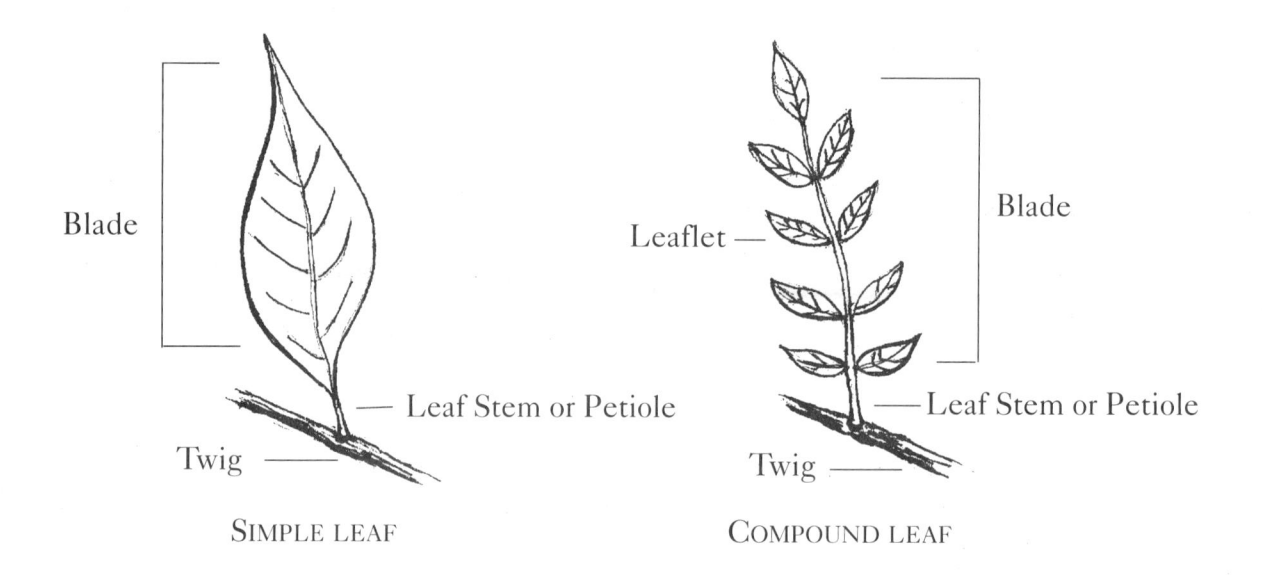

SIMPLE LEAF

COMPOUND LEAF

Leaves are attached to the twig in three ways:

OPPOSITE   ALTERNATE   WHORLED

Leaves grow in many sizes and shapes. Some shapes are easy to remember—their names are based on shapes that are already familiar to you.

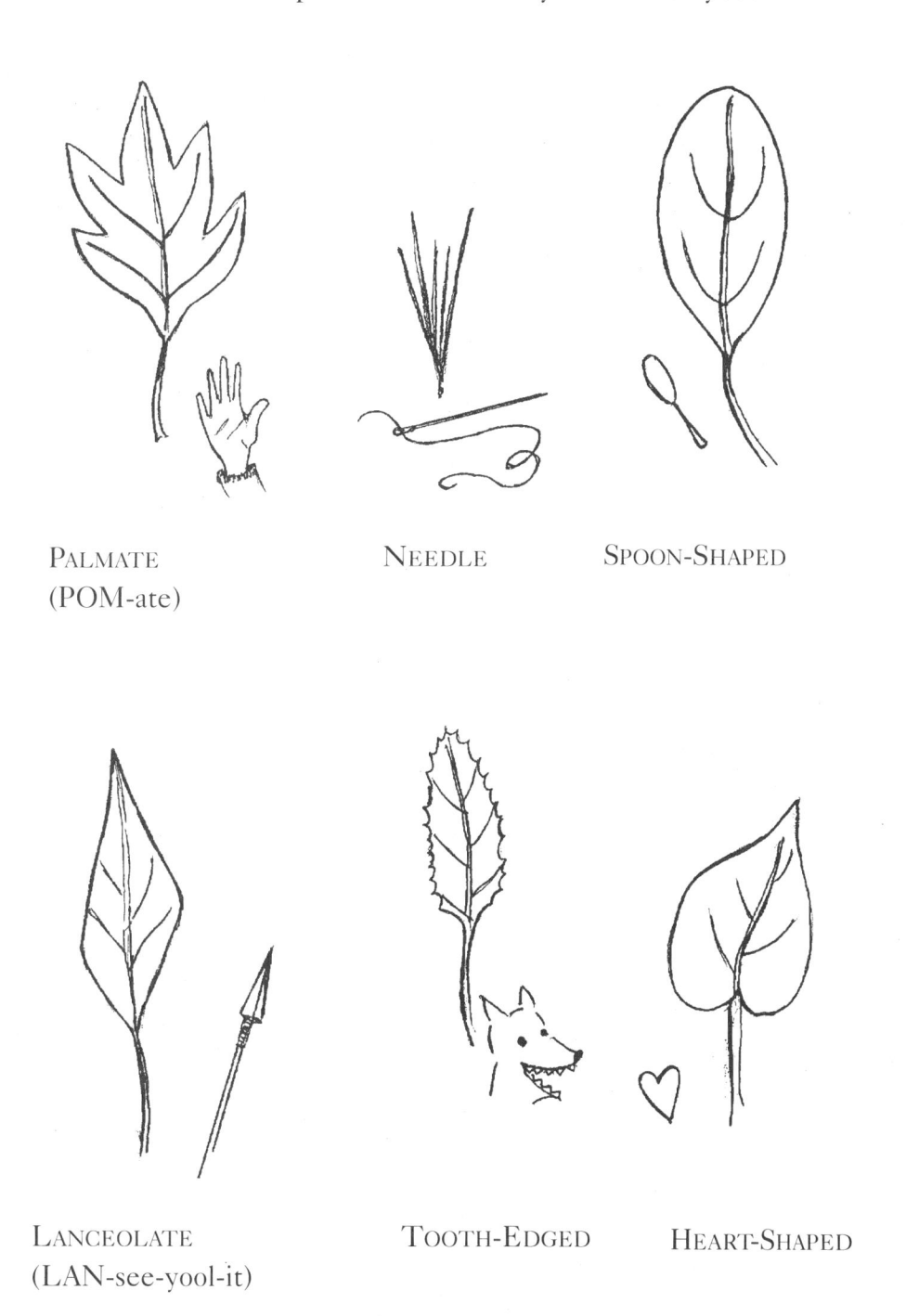

PALMATE
(POM-ate)

NEEDLE

SPOON-SHAPED

LANCEOLATE
(LAN-see-yool-it)

TOOTH-EDGED

HEART-SHAPED

Tree Flowers and Fruits

Most trees have flowers. When the flower dies, a fruit is left in its place. The fruit contains a seed. When the seed is planted, it sprouts and grows into a tree.

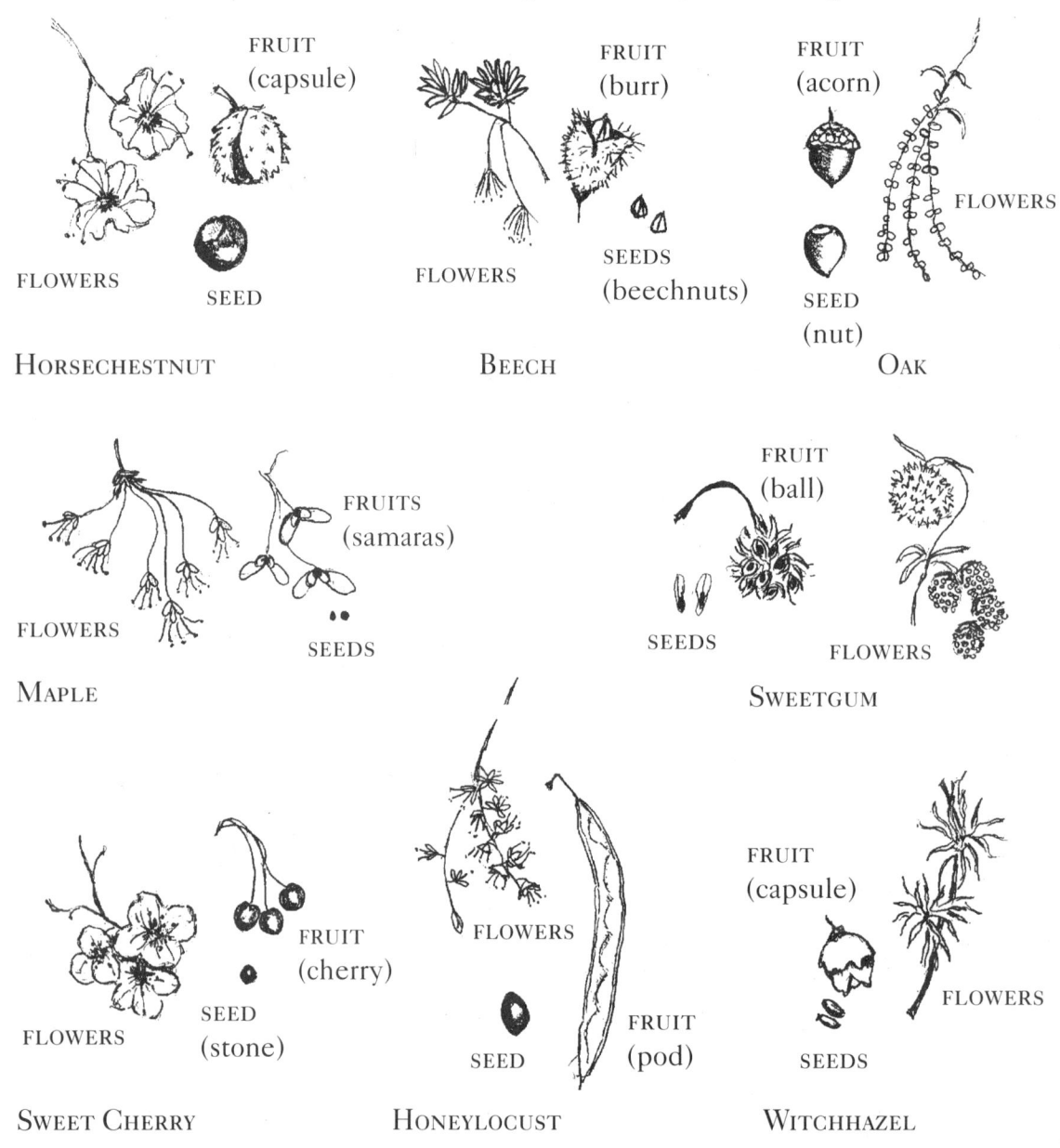

FRUIT (capsule)
FLOWERS
SEED
Horsechestnut

FRUIT (burr)
FLOWERS
SEEDS (beechnuts)
Beech

FRUIT (acorn)
FLOWERS
SEED (nut)
Oak

FRUITS (samaras)
FLOWERS
SEEDS
Maple

FRUIT (ball)
SEEDS
FLOWERS
Sweetgum

FLOWERS
SEED (stone)
FRUIT (cherry)
Sweet Cherry

FLOWERS
SEED
FRUIT (pod)
Honeylocust

FRUIT (capsule)
SEEDS
FLOWERS
Witchhazel

Instead of flowers, the group of trees called conifers (CON-ih-furs)—evergreen trees such as pines—have two kinds of cones: pollen cones and seed cones.

In the spring powdery pollen is released from the pollen cones. The wind carries the pollen, and some of it lands on seed cones. At this stage some seed cones are tinier than ladybugs. Then the seeds, protected by the cone's scales, begin to grow bigger.

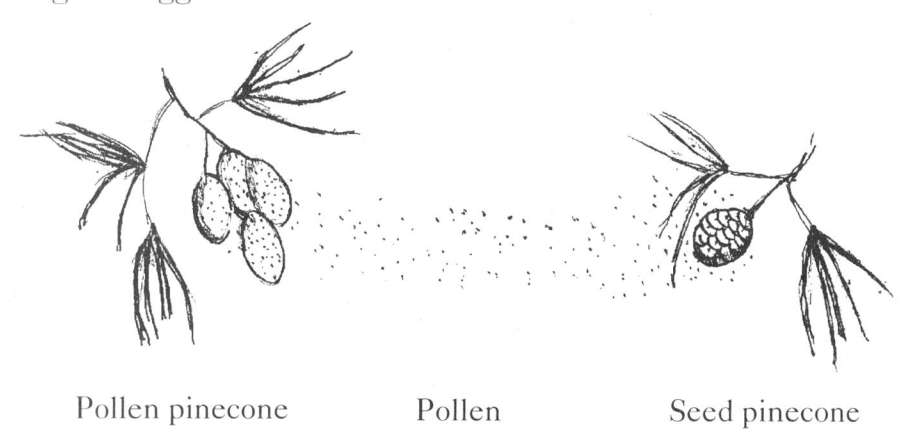

Pollen pinecone	Pollen	Seed pinecone

Seed pinecones take two or three years to fully grow. Then the scales open up and free the seeds. Each seed has a papery covering. Like a tiny wing, it's carried by the wind. If it lands on the right kind of soil, it sprouts into a seedling, then eventually grows into a tall pine tree.

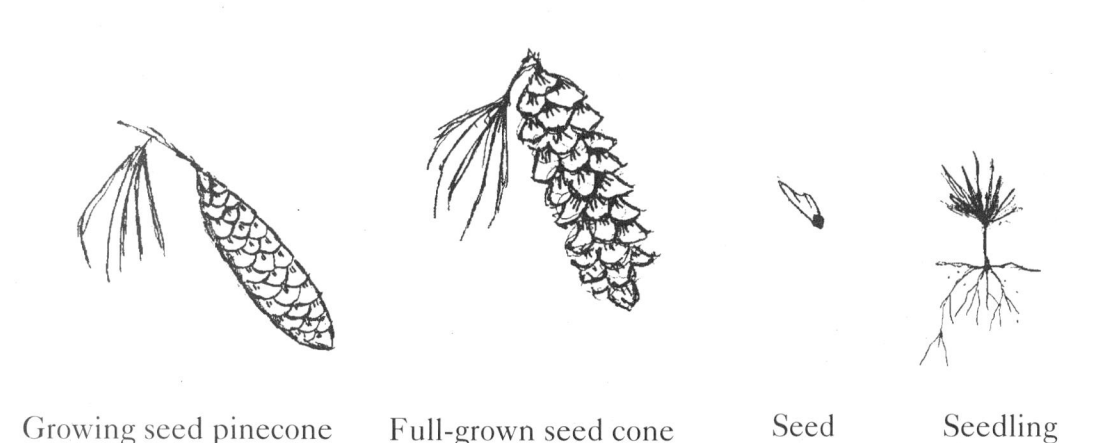

Growing seed pinecone	Full-grown seed cone	Seed	Seedling

A Close Look at Bark and What's Behind It

Bark protects the tree's insides from disease and insects. Some bark is almost fireproof.

The wood in the center of a tree is called the heartwood. It's the oldest wood and it's also dead. The living wood grows in layers or rings around the heartwood. Each year a new ring of wood grows in the inner bark, a *very* thin layer right behind the outer bark (the bark that you see).

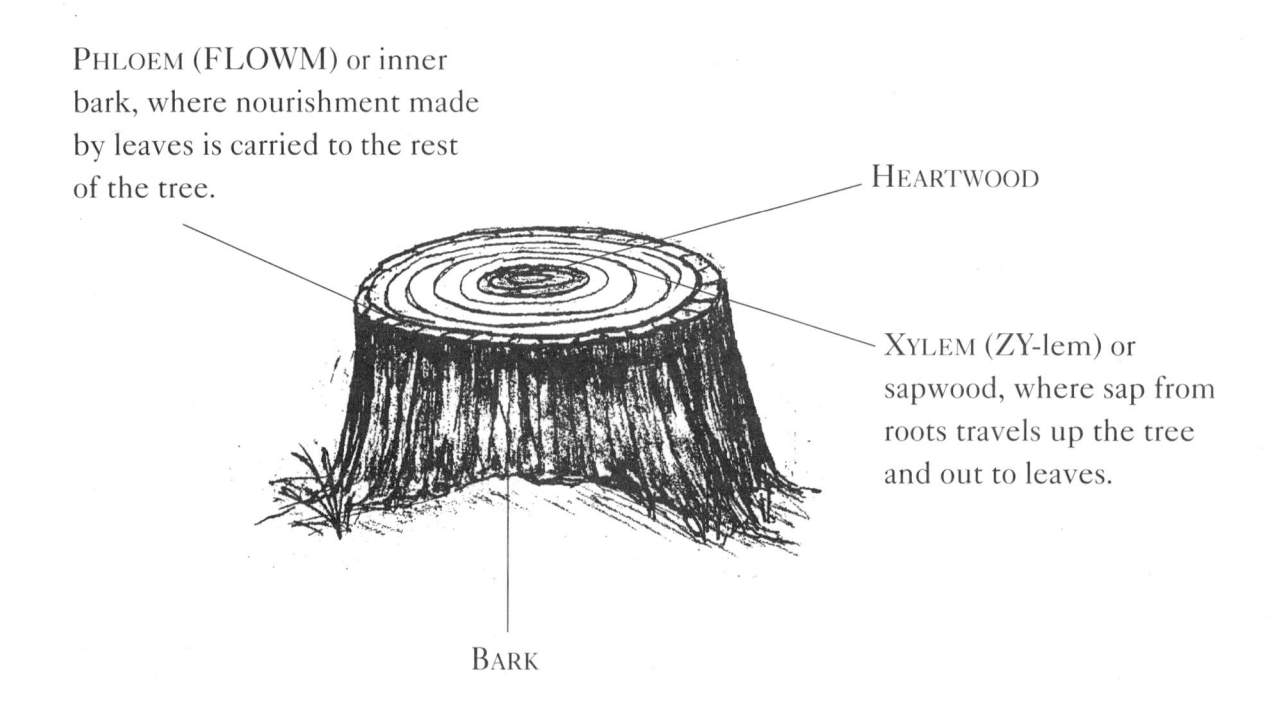

PHLOEM (FLOWM) or inner bark, where nourishment made by leaves is carried to the rest of the tree.

HEARTWOOD

XYLEM (ZY-lem) or sapwood, where sap from roots travels up the tree and out to leaves.

BARK

Each kind of tree has its own bark. It may be as thick as a slice of bread or thinner than paper. Bark can be gray, reddish, brown, yellowish, or green. Bark can peel, be covered with bumps or deep grooves, or feel smooth.

SYCAMORE

SWAMP WHITE OAK

HONEYLOCUST

PERSIMMON

SOUR CHERRY

APPLE

SAUCER MAGNOLIA

PAPER-MULBERRY

SHAGBARK HICKORY

Become a Tree Detective

In winter when trees are bare, you might think they look dead and not very pretty. And without leaves, how can you tell one kind of tree from another?

This is the time to become a tree detective!

BRANCHING PATTERN AND OUTLINE CLUES

Each kind of tree has its own outline or branching pattern. You can see it against the sky. Tree experts can recognize a tree from far away by just looking at the branching pattern. By looking at branching patterns, you'll also see how beautiful trees can be without leaves.

These tree shapes are easy to recognize. They look like their names.

VASE-SHAPED OUTLINE
Looks like a flower vase.

COLUMNAR OUTLINE
Straight up and down like a column.

WEEPING OUTLINE
Drooping, "sad."

FRUIT CLUES

If a tree has an acorn lying close by, it may not be an oak. A squirrel might have dropped it. But if a tree has an acorn hanging from a branch, you'll know it's an oak!

Sweetgum ball   Honeylocust pod   Maple samara   Oak acorn

LEAF BUD CLUES

Leaf buds grow in a certain way on each kind of tree.

Horsechestnut   Elm   White Oak

BARK CLUES

Some barks are hard to recognize. But if you see a smooth-barked tree, you can be sure it's not a shagbark hickory.

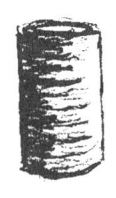

Beech   Shagbark Hickory

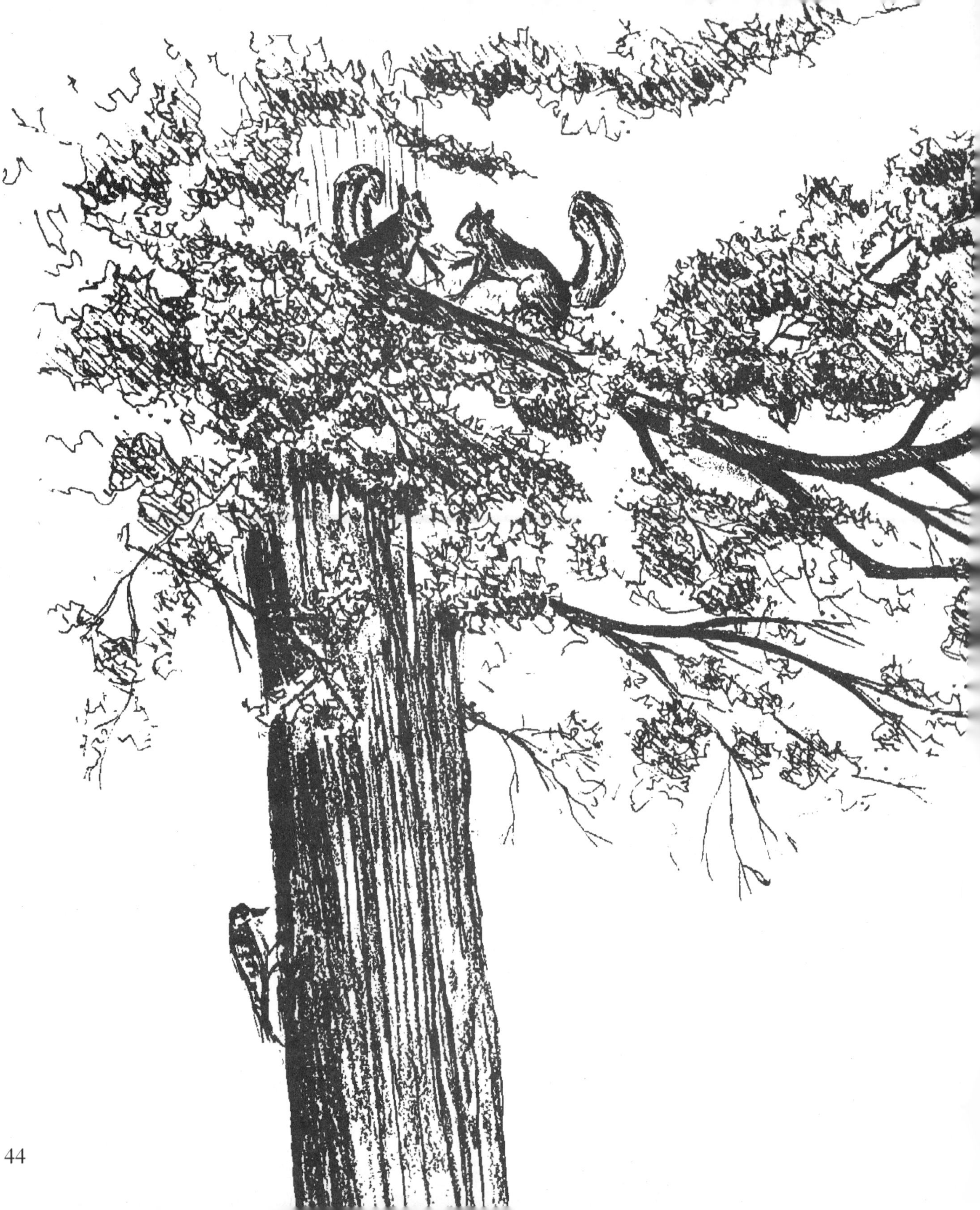

Tree Dwellers

A tree is a *very* popular hangout.

Birds find nesting spots among its branches or in hollows in the trunk. When the tree's flowers bloom, crowds of bees and butterflies drink the nectar hidden in the blossoms.

All kinds of leaf-eating insects find plenty to munch. They nibble their way from leaf to leaf. But hungry birds also poke among the leaves and feast on the nibbling insects.

At night a tree can be a pretty noisy place. Cicadas, crickets, and tiny frogs fill the air with croaks and chirps and rasping sounds. But quiet creatures are also wide awake. Through moonlit branches, moths flutter, bats swoop, and owls glide on silent wings.

And every tree is bound to have squirrels. On any given day, you're sure to see them chasing one another up and down the branches. Trees don't only provide them with food and shelter—for squirrels, a tree makes a great playground.

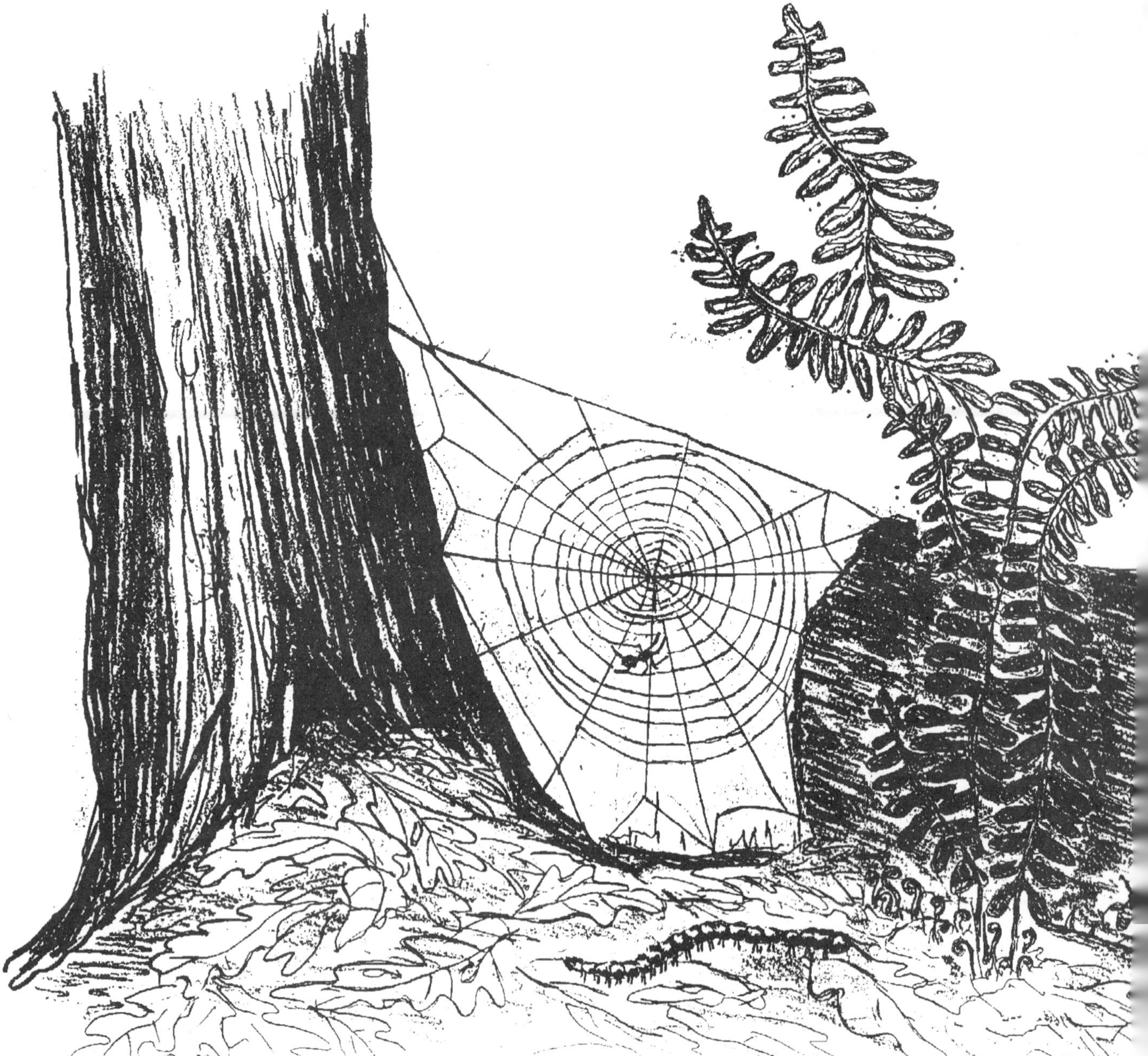

Who's Hiding on the Floor?

The ground beneath woodland trees is called the forest floor. When animals such as deer, skunks, or raccoons aren't around, it might look like a pretty dull place. But it's not. Amid the rotting logs and dead leaves, there's plenty going on.

Like trees, the forest floor provides food and a place to live for a variety of creatures. It also provides the rich soil that nourishes the trees. As the dead leaves and fallen trees rot away, they add nutrients to the soil. When it rains or snows, the nutrients sink into the ground. Then they're absorbed by roots and carried up into the living trees.

Many forest-floor insects tunnel through decaying logs and tree stumps searching for food. Termites—insects that look like big whitish ants—actually eat dead wood. This makes the wood break down more quickly. And the sooner the wood breaks down, the sooner it turns into soil.

So while the forest floor's tiny insects are feeding themselves, they are also helping to feed the trees.

Tracks in the Snow

A deer track in snow is easy to identify. It looks like the bottom of the deer's hoof. But some animals' wintry tracks don't look anything like their footprints. Their strange-looking tracks show how they travel through the snow.

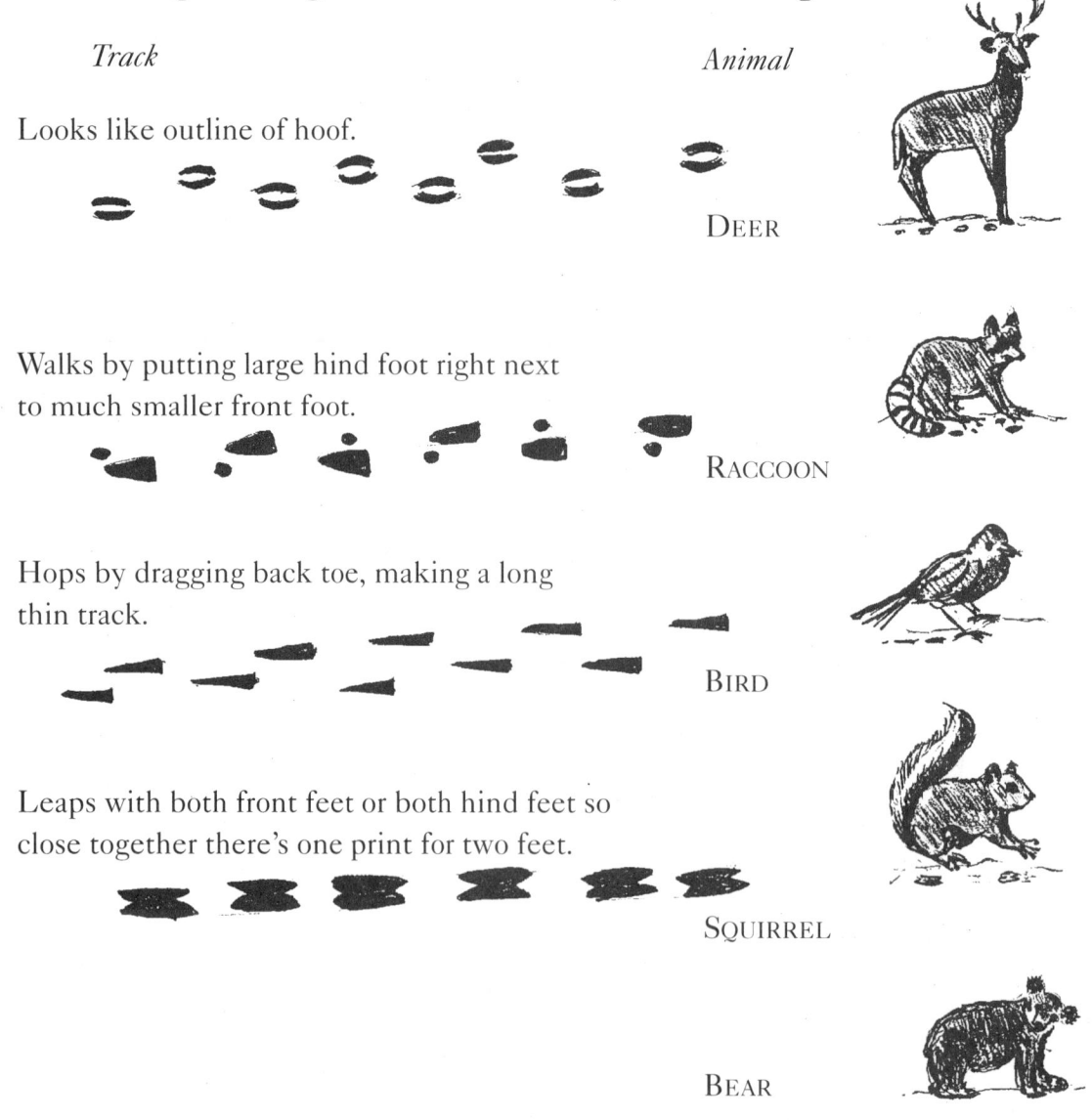

Track *Animal*

Looks like outline of hoof.

DEER

Walks by putting large hind foot right next to much smaller front foot.

RACCOON

Hops by dragging back toe, making a long thin track.

BIRD

Leaps with both front feet or both hind feet so close together there's one print for two feet.

SQUIRREL

BEAR

Where are the bear's tracks? Bears hibernate—that means they sleep through the winter. They can't leave tracks if they're asleep!

That's a Snowflake?

During a snowstorm, snowflakes all look the same. But if you looked at them under a magnifying glass, you'd see something pretty amazing.

    A snowflakes starts out as a tiny speck of dust or sea salt. When it blows around it might be carried up to the sky. There it attracts water droplets from clouds. When the air is very cold, the droplets form ice around the little speck. It grows into a shape called a crystal. The shapes depend upon the kind of clouds. During one snowfall, the shapes of the crystals may change.

STELLAR CRYSTAL

COLUMN CRYSTAL

NEEDLE CRYSTAL

SIX-SIDED PLATE CRYSTAL

GRAUPEL

    Look closely at snowflakes as they fall on your glove. You can see some crystals without a magnifying glass.

Wildflowers

Found in Shady Woods

Smooth Solomon's Seal
Eight inches to 3 feet tall. Greenish white flowers.

Shooting Star
Eight to 20 inches tall. Pink or white flower.

Jack-in-the-Pulpit
One to 3 feet tall. Green or purplish brown flower.

Trillium (TRILL-ee-um)
Eight to 18 inches tall. White flower.

Yellow Lady's Slipper
Four to 28 inches tall. Yellow flower.

Wild Mint
Six inches to 2 feet tall. Lavender or white flower.

Found in Sunny Fields

FLEABANE
Six inches to 3 feet tall. White or pink flower with large yellow center.

BLACK-EYED SUSAN
One to 3 feet tall. Yellow flower with brown center.

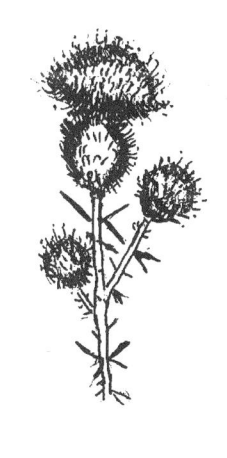

BULL THISTLE (THISS-ull)
Two to 6 feet tall. Red-purple flower.

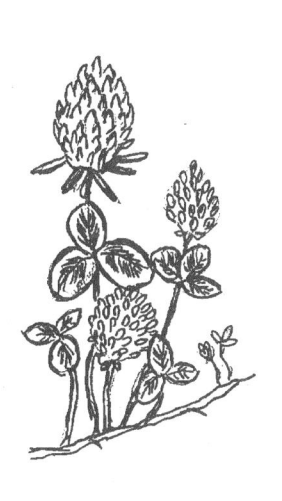

WHITE CLOVER
Four to 10 inches tall. White or pinkish flower.

LUPINE (LOO-pin)
Eight inches to 2 feet tall. Blue flower.

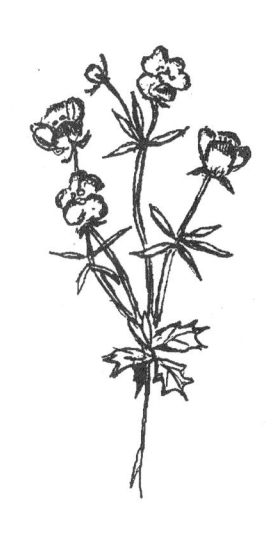

BUTTERCUP
Two to 3 feet tall. Yellow flower.

Fern: Two Plants in One

In the spring feathery-looking fern plants appear in the woodlands. At first they're tightly curled. At this stage they're called fiddleheads because they look like the end of a violin or fiddle. The fiddleheads unwind into a frond—a leaf stalk supporting hundreds of tiny leaflets called pinnae (PIN-ee). In the fall the fern fronds turn brown and wither away.

Ferns don't have flowers. Instead of seeds, dustlike spores develop inside spore sacs on the backs on the pinnae. The sacs look like tiny brown bumps.

During dry autumn days the sacs split and shoot the spores into the air. But when they fall to the ground, a feathery fern doesn't start to grow.

First, a flat heart-shaped plant appears. It's called a prothallus (pro-THALL-us) and is about the size of a dime. It contains two kinds of cells—sperm cells and egg cells. Nothing happens until the prothallus gets wet (from rain or dew). Then the sperm cells float across the plant and fertilize the egg cells. A new tiny fern plant grows from each fertilized egg cell.

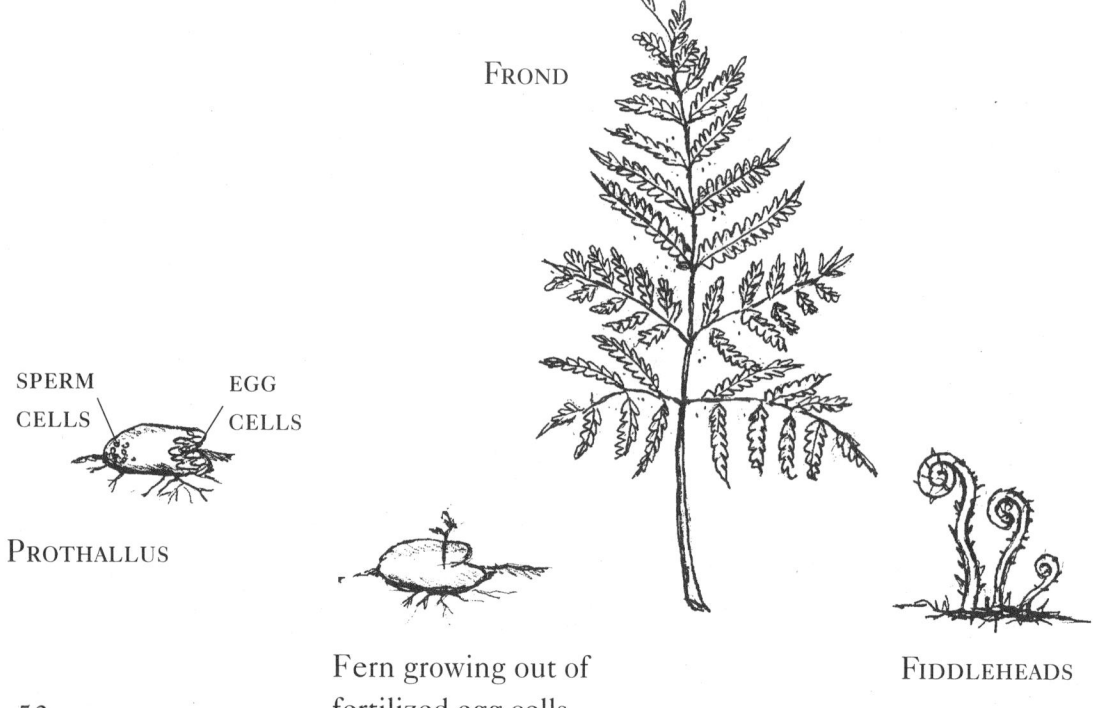

FROND

SPERM CELLS / EGG CELLS

PROTHALLUS

Fern growing out of fertilized egg cells.

FIDDLEHEADS

Mushrooms: They Can't Live Alone!

Full-grown mushrooms often appear overnight. It seems like magic. Where do they come from?

Mushrooms are the fruits of a plant called a fungus (FUNG-us). Some underground fungi (FUNG-eye—the plural of *fungus*) can spread for hundreds of acres.

A fungus is white or grayish. Because it doesn't contain the green substance called chlorophyll (KLOR-oh-fill), it can't make its own food. It has to live off other plants.

Fungi live off underground tree roots, bark, dead leaves, and old logs. Because they don't rely on chlorophyll, mushrooms can even grow in the dark.

Like ferns, mushrooms contain spores. They may be pink, purple, white, black, or brown. If a spore falls near something it can live on, it forms a long thready growth, and a new fungus begins to grow.

Be careful! Some mushrooms are poisonous. Wash your hands if you handle them. *Never eat any mushrooms you find growing in the woods!*

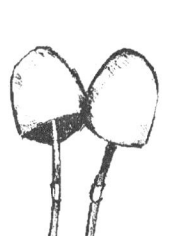

HORSEHAIR FUNGUS

HALF-EGG

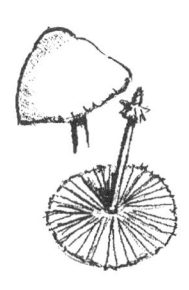

FAIRY RING

BOHEMIAN (Bo-HEE-me-an)

CUP-SHAPED

PARASOL

ERECT

CHANTERELLE (shan-tuh-RELL)

Cap — Gills — Ring — Spores

Birds, Birds, Birds!

Everywhere you go for a walk—through woods, across a field, down city streets—you're sure to see birds. Here are a dozen that live in many parts of the United States.

Junco (JUNK-o)
Five to 6 1/2 inches long.
Gray and white.

Blue Jay
Twelve inches long.
Blue and white. Loud J call.

Cardinal
Eight inches long.
Male: Bright red.
Female: Olive green.

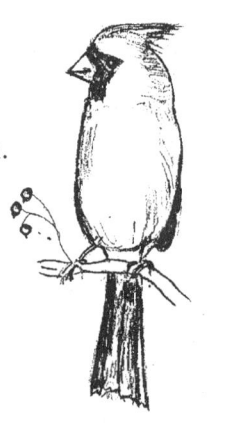

American Goldfinch
Four and a half to 5 inches long.
Bright yellow, black cap, black wings.

Hermit Thrush
Six and a half to 8 inches long.
Spotted breast.
Beautiful flutelike call.

Tufted Titmouse
Six inches long.
Feathered tuft on top of head.

White-Breasted Nuthatch
Five to 6 inches long.
Often climbs down headfirst on tree trunks.

Ruby-Throated Hummingbird
Three and a half inches long.
Tiny bird. Wings make faint buzzing sound. Drinks flower nectar with long bill.

Black-Capped Chickadee
Four and a quarter to 5 3/4 inches long.
Often eats hanging upside down.

American Robin
Nine to 11 inches long.
Grayish black back, orange breast.

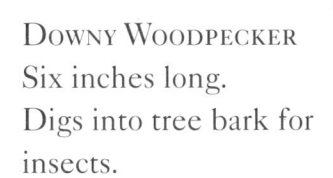

Downy Woodpecker
Six inches long.
Digs into tree bark for insects.

Northern Mockingbird
Nine to 11 inches long.
Long tail. In flight, white patch seen on wings. Mimics songs of other birds.

Trees Today . . .

We make use of all parts of a tree.

It's easy to guess how some wood is used. Firewood is burned for heat and sometimes for cooking food. We build wood houses and furniture. You can probably think of many other wooden products, such as pencils and toys.

Cellulose (SELL-yoo-lohs), the main part of wood, is ground into pulp and manufactured into paper. It's also used in making suntan lotion, shatterproof glass, and cosmetics.

Bees make honey from tree flowers. Many people eat honey. We also get fruits from trees: apples, pears, dates, peaches, coconuts, oranges, bananas, plums, olives, and cherries, to name just a few. Nuts, cocoa, and coffee beans also come from trees.

Sap from the sugar maple tree is boiled into maple syrup. But did you know other tree saps are used in making rubber, chewing gum, and shoe polish?

Medicines are made from some trees' leaves and bark. Many were known hundreds of years ago. But today, plant scientists are finding new ones. They think trees and other plants may hold the cures for many diseases.

. . . And Tomorrow

Every year in the United States, millions of trees are cut down for our use. Every day thousands of trees are destroyed just to make newspapers and magazines. A lot of paper is used once and thrown away. This terrible waste has been going on for years. What can we do before all the trees disappear?

Here are three ways people are trying to prevent the loss of our great American forests:

RECYCLE
Old paper is being recycled (processed) into new paper. Scientists are also trying to come up with new ways to recycle unwanted used wood.

REPLANT
Timber companies replace the trees they cut down. As the trees are removed, seedlings are planted. They will grow into trees to be used in the future.

PROTECT
Some woodlands are protected by law. At present, there are places where trees can't be damaged or destroyed.

A woodland is more than a lot of trees. It's more than a home to animals—or a spot where wildflowers grow—or a trail for you to hike.

It's a place that is able to renew itself. Left alone, a woodland continues on, creating new growth from old and providing for all the creatures that live there.

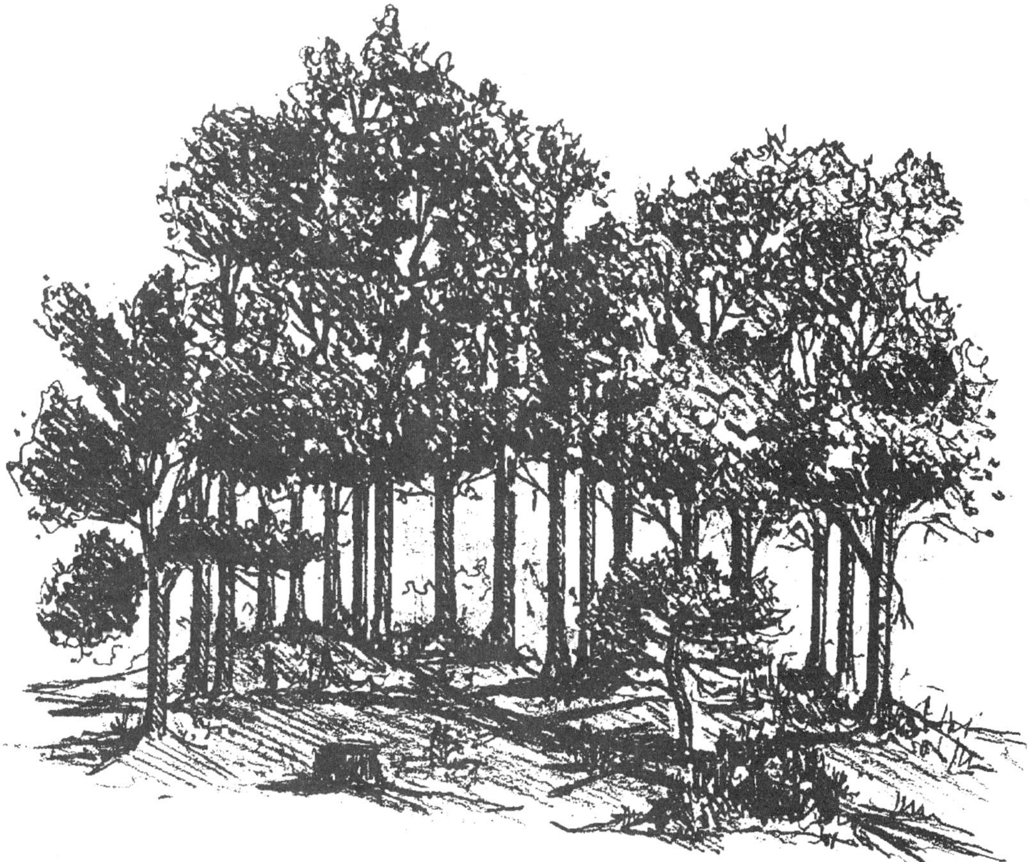

Tips for the Nature Trail

Going on a nature walk is one of the nicest things you can do. To have a safe time and get the most out of your walk, follow these tips.

- Carry a light backpack containing the following items:
    - A notebook. You can press leaves and flowers between the pages, make notes about your walk, or sketch what you see.
    - A small flashlight. At certain times of the year, it gets dark very quickly.
    - A snack and a plastic bottle of water (plastic is lighter than glass). If you carry your own water, you'll *know* it's safe to drink.
- Always take a friend with you when you set out on a woodland walk.
- Even if it's hot when you set out, tie a sweatshirt or light jacket around your waist in case it gets cool later in the day.
- If it's buggy, wear long pants instead of shorts.
- Dab some sunscreen on your face, ears, neck, and arms. You can get sunburned even on a cloudy day.
- Wear comfortable shoes. There's nothing worse than walking around on sore feet!
- Stay on the marked trail. If the trail divides, look around for a landmark. Then on the way back, you'll recognize it and know which way to turn.
- Learn how to read a compass. Then you'll know which direction you're going. If you don't have a compass, just remember that the sun rises in the east and sets in the west. If you face the setting sun and hold out your arms, your right arm will be pointing north and your left arm will be pointing south.

- Do you want to know which way the wind is blowing? Put your finger in your mouth, then hold it up. The wind will make your finger feel cold. The side of your finger that feels coldest is the direction the wind is coming from.
- Look all around you as you walk. Compare tree barks. What shapes are the clouds? Do you see any animal tracks?
- If you hear thunder in the distance, head for home immediately or find a good shelter.
- Make sure you don't leave any litter behind. If there aren't any trash containers along the trail, carry your trash home and throw it away there.
- Every now and then just stand still and listen. You'll be surprised at how many sounds you'll hear—birds, insects buzzing, the wind, rushing water.
- If you ever get lost, don't start wandering around. Stay right where you are. That will make it easier for someone to find you.

Index

Acorns, 28, 38, 43
Anthocyanins, 33
Apples, 41, 56
Arborvitae, giant, 17
Ash, white, 8, 32

Bark, 12, 16, 18, 20, 24, 40, 43, 53
Basswood, 10, 32
Bears, 28, 48
Bees, 10, 45, 56
Beech, 38, 43
Bee-tree, 10, 11, 32
Birch
   canoe, 13, 32
   paper, 12, 32
   white, 13
Birds, 18, 22, 45, 48, 54
Black-eyed Susan, 51
Bohemian mushroom, 53
Bract, 10, 18
Burrs, 38
Buttercup, 51
Butternut, 14

Capsules, 38
Carbon dioxide, 34
Cardinal, 54
Carotenoids, 33
Cellulose, 56
Chanterelle, 53
Cherry
   sour, 41
   sweet, 38
Chickadee, black-capped, 55
Chlorophyll, 7, 33, 53
Clover, white, 51
Cones, 30, 39
Conifer, 39
Cup-shaped mushroom, 53

Deer, 28, 47, 48
Dogwood, flowering, 18

Elm, 43
   moose, 21
   red, 21
   slippery, 20
Erect mushroom, 53

Fairy ring, 53
Fascicle, 30
Ferns, 52, 53
Fiddleheads, 52
Fleabane, 51
Floor, forest, 47
Flowers, tree, 38, 56
Frond, 52
Fruits, 8, 10, 18, 20, 22, 24, 26, 30, 38, 43
Fungus, 53

Ginkgo, 33
Goldfinch, American, 54

Half-egg mushroom, 53
Hawthorn, cockspur, 22
Heartwood, 40
Hickory, shagbark, 24, 41, 43
Honeylocust, 33, 38, 41, 43
Hornbeam, 33
Horsechestnut, 38, 43
Horsehair fungus, 53
Hummingbird, ruby-throated, 55

Insects, 40, 45, 47

Jack-in-the-pulpit, 50
Jay, blue, 54
Junco, 54

Kernaes, 24, 28

Lady's slipper, yellow, 50
Leaves, 33
   alternate, 36
   blade, 36
   bud, 43
   compound, 24, 36
   decaying, 47, 53
   heart-shaped, 37
   lanceolate, 37
   needle, 16, 30, 37
   opposite, 36

palmate, 37
simple, 36
spoon-shaped, 37
stem, 36
tooth-edged, 22, 37
whorled, 36
Linden, American, 11, 32
Lupine, 51

Magnolia, saucer, 41
Maple, 38, 43
  hard, 27
  rock, 27
  sugar, 26, 33, 56
Mint, wild, 50
Mockingbird, northern, 55
Mulberry, paper, 41
Mushrooms, 53

Name, common, 32
Name, scientific, 32
Nuts, 24, 38, 56
Nuthatch, white-breasted, 55

Oak, 38, 43
  red, 28
  scarlet, 33
  swamp white, 41
  white, 43
Oilnut, 15
Oxygen, 34

Parasol mushroom, 53

Persimmon, 41
Petiole, 36
Phloem, 40
Photosynthesis, 7
Pine, eastern white, 30
Pinnae, 52
Pods, 38, 43
Pollen, 34, 39
Prothallus, 52

Raccoon, 47, 48
Recycling, 57
Red cedar, western, 16
Robin, American, 55
Roots, 7, 16, 18, 34, 47, 53

Samara, 8, 20, 26
Sap, 7, 12, 26, 40, 56
Sassafras, 33
Seeds, 20, 24, 30, 38, 39, 52
Seedling, 39, 57
Shooting star, 50
Snow crystals, 49
Snowflake, 49
Soil, 34, 39, 47

Solomon's seal, smooth, 50
Squirrel, 28, 45, 48
Sweetgum, 33, 38, 43
Sycamore, 41

Termites, 47
Thistle, bull, 51
Thorns, 22
Thrush, hermit, 54
Tracks, 47
Trillium, 50
Tufted titmouse, 54
Tulip tree, 33

Walnut, white, 15
Windbreaks, 34
Witchhazel, 38
Woodpecker, downy, 55

Xylem, 40

Author and illustrator GINA INGOGLIA has written more than seventy books for children. She holds a degree in landscape architecture from Rutgers University and is a member of the American Society of Landscape Architects and the Garden Writers of America. Her column, "The Budding Gardener," is published by the Brooklyn Botanic Garden. She and her husband, Earl Weiner, live in Brooklyn Heights, New York. They have two grown children.